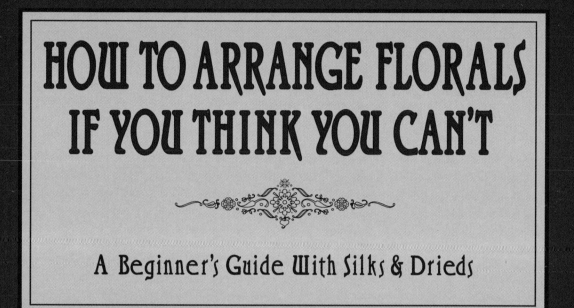

HOW TO ARRANGE FLORALS IF YOU THINK YOU CAN'T

A Beginner's Guide With Silks & Drieds

The publisher and designer wish to thank the following companies for providing materials used in this publication:

- ❀ **Adhesive Technologies, Inc.** for low temperature glue gun and sticks
- ❀ **Aleene's/Artis Inc.** for tacky craft glue
- ❀ **American Oak Preserving Co.** for dried materials, grapevine and pine cone wreaths
- ❀ **C.M. Offray & Son, Inc.** for ribbon
- ❀ **Colorado Evergreen Import Co.** for birch bark tubes
- ❀ **Decorator & Craft Corp.** for papier-mâché boxes and reindeer
- ❀ **Delta Technical Coatings** for acrylic paints, wood stain gels
- ❀ **Design Master color tool, inc.** for wood tone glossy stains
- ❀ **Fiberex, Inc.** for American Moss® excelsior
- ❀ **Frontier Imports, Inc.** for baskets, log items, topiaries
- ❀ **International Flower Imports, Inc.** for dried flowers, greenery and pods
- ❀ **Lion Ribbon Co., Inc.** for ribbon, cord and braid
- ❀ **Luzon Imports** for all TWIGS™ items, baskets
- ❀ **MPR Associates, Inc.** for twisted satin ribbon
- ❀ **Panacea Products Corp.** for floral wire
- ❀ **Robert Simmons, Inc.** for paintbrushes
- ❀ **Schusters Of Texas, Inc.** for feathers, dried flowers, fruits, pods, cones, and mushrooms
- ❀ **Smithers-Oasis USA** for glue pan and pellets, floral foam for silk and dried flowers
- ❀ **Sopp America, Inc.** for ribbon
- ❀ **Teter's Floral Products, Inc.** for silk and latex stems, bushes, pine garlands, wreaths, swags and stems, fall and Christmas picks
- ❀ **Walnut Hollow** for wood shelves
- ❀ **Wang's International, Inc.** for silk and latex stems and picks, twig garlands, baskets, root wreaths, Halloween cats, birdhouses and vine swags
- ❀ **Winward Silks** for silk and latex flowers, berries, fruits and greenery
- ❀ **W.J. Cowee, Inc.** for wired wood picks

About the Designer...

Teresa Nelson is the master designer and vice president of Hot Off The Press. She has written over 50 books on floral design, weddings, appliqué, fabric painting, jewelry making and gift wrapping. Her books have sold over one million copies world-wide.

We are proud to have this very talented lady designing exclusively for Hot Off The Press. Thank you, Teresa!

Dedicated to Paulette and Mike Jarvey:

Your friendship and encouragement have compelled me to grow in directions I might otherwise have overlooked. (And, at times, I'm sure it's been very entertaining!) Thank you for your patience, understanding and especially your love. Please know you are loved in return.

Production Credits:

Project editor: Mary Margaret Hite
Technical editor: LeNae Gerig
Photographer: Meredith Marsh
Graphic designer: Sally Clarke
Digital imagers: Shawn Jarvey, Michael Kincaid
Editors: Paulette Jarvey, Tom Muir

published by:

P.O. Box 5595
Little Rock, Arkansas 72215

produced by:

HOW TO ARRANGE FLORALS IF YOU THINK YOU CAN'T

A Beginner's Guide With Silks & Drieds

TABLE OF CONTENTS

IDENTIFICATION OF FLOWERS & MATERIALS

Walking into a floral department in a craft store can be so overwhelming if you aren't prepared for what you'll see or if you're not sure of what you need. Our list of materials needed for each project should help, but what if you don't know the difference between a latex and a silk flower? This section has photos of the most commonly used materials in flower-arranging with a short explanation of their properties. While not every store carries every stem used in the book, knowledge of what you're searching for will help should you need to substitute stems.

Silk Flowers

Because "silk" flowers aren't actually made from silk, but from polyester, they hold their shapes well; some are actually weatherproof. The quality of polysilks has greatly improved, with more realistic flowers being created. Natural colors are used, with shading or veining in the petals to make them more botanically correct.

"Dried-Silk" Flowers

These are polysilk flowers, but with curled edges which make them look dried.

Delores Ruzicka, a designer in Nebraska, has discovered a method of turning regular polysilks into dried silks which she calls "flower zapping." Hold the flower by the stem in one hand; direct the heat from a heat gun or paint stripper onto the petals and leaves, being extremely careful not to burn yourself. Begin on a low temperature setting to acquaint yourself with the process.

Zapping stems of polysilk leaves makes them more realistic. Orange, yellow and brown autumn leaves, as well as regular green leaves, once zapped, can become very attractive additions to floral designs.

Hand-Wrapped Flowers

Most elegant silk and parchment flowers are actually hand-wrapped, meaning they're assembled by hand and the stems are wrapped with floral tape. Their stems can be hard to cut, because the flowers and leaves are on separate wire stems which are wrapped together onto a heavy wire, but they're beautiful.

Of course, the more effort put into producing the flowers, the more expensive they become. However, a design using the higher-quality, more realistic flowers can be enjoyed much longer than the less expensive polysilks; they will be in style longer with their colors spanning more seasons.

Foam Flowers:

Brand new on the scene are foam flowers, constructed of high-density, very thin foam. Usually, as is the case with the flowers shown, the leaves or thicker parts of the flowers are foam with the blossom being polysilk. The results are blossoms and leaves which are extremely realistic to view and touch.

In an effort to make silk flowers more botanically correct and to add visual interest to arrangements, manufacturers are creating flowers with bulbs and roots attached. The only limitation to using these is they must be left intact, making it difficult to achieve varying heights in the design. They are wonderful to use and add another level of realism.

Fabric Flowers:

Non-woven fabric is used to make these flowers. It is cut and shaped into petals, which are then hand-wrapped together. The leaves usually include wires to shape them, and the petals are shaded for more realism. These flowers have an upscale look because of the veins and ridges pressed into the petals as well as the muted colors achieved in the finishing process.

Latex Flowers

Parchment and silk flowers that have a cool, rubbery feel have been dipped in latex. They're realistic to touch and add an elegant look to an arrangement.

Keep latex flowers from becoming overheated as the latex can soften and become sticky. Store in a cool, dry place.

Dried Materials

Many unique dried flowers and materials are available—we're not limited just to straw flowers and baby's breath any more! Air-dried flowers can be very delicate and should be handled with care.

"Preserved" flowers fall into the dried flower category. They have been preserved with glycerine and are a bit hardier than dried flowers. They have a waxy feel to them and do not shatter as easily. (See "Drying Your Own Flowers," page 27, for more information.)

Silk Bushes

These are available in many configurations, as flowering plants or as greenery with varying numbers of sprigs attached to one main stem. The sprigs may also be varied in length on one stem, making the bush look realistic.

Some bushes include more than one type of flower or plant. These are fun to work with, since the colors are already coordinated for you—plus they may be less expensive to use!

Of course the more sprigs on a plant stem, the more expensive it becomes. And with more sprigs to work with, a fuller, lusher design can be made.

To use a bush, either insert it as a plant in a design, or cut the sprigs off the main stem and insert individually. Sprigs may also be cut apart and attached to a wreath or basket rim.

Flowering Vines & Garlands

Different types of flowers and plants come as vines. They vary in lengths from 30" to 9 feet. These are convenient if a long garland is required.

Garlands can be a base for other materials such as dried or silk blossoms. Dip the flower stem ends in hot glue and insert them among the garland leaves or flowers, making sure they are glued to the main stem.

Pine or Fir Garlands

PVC or vinyl garlands commonly come in 9-foot lengths and are very versatile. They can be cut into shorter lengths and wired to baskets, wreaths or other bases.

It can be quicker and easier to use a garland rather than stems for designing. A pine garland wired to a grapevine wreath is a great start for a Christmas wreath. Or, if pine stems are needed but none are on hand, make them by cutting 8–12-sprig sections of pine garland and wiring each to a long wood pick.

To cut a garland, spread apart the individual sprigs and cut through the heavy binding wires; twist the cut wire ends together to secure the sprigs nearest the ends.

Picks

Floral picks are short stems of clustered items. Christmas picks, the most common, may include berries, cones, silk leaves, packages, ornaments, pine sprigs, etc. Short (4"–7" tall) stems of flowers or greenery are also called picks; they are very inexpensive. Flower picks generally include 1–3 blossoms with several leaves per stem. Greenery picks can be small plants, such as violets, or just leaves on a stem; these look especially nice clustered in a woodsy basket.

While picks can be effective inserted as stems, they can also be cut into individual components. Attach each to a wood pick, then insert into the design in a scattered pattern.

Fruits & Vegetables

These have become important elements in floral designing. They are available in polysilk, vinyl, freeze-dried or air-dried. When dried fruit slices are used in design work, each is attached by gluing a U-pin to the bottom of the slice, then inserting into the foam. For whole fruits and vegetables, glue one end of a pick into the piece, making a stem.

Berry Stems

Stems of grapes and smooth round berries have remained popular, adding texture or becoming fillers in a design. More intricate berries and vines are also available. They can look good enough to eat and are wonderful additions to arrangements, adding color, shine, and unique textures.

Berries are available as picks, on stems or as vines. They come with or without leaves and can even be found mixed in with flowers or bushes on the same stem. Berries are fun to include in woodsy designs, adding a wild, natural look.

Pods & Mushrooms

It's easy to find many varieties of pods, with a wide range of sizes, colors and textures. Gold or silver painted pods can add a touch of shine to a Christmas design. Dried tree fungus, also known as dried mushrooms, are a realistic addition to the woodsy, natural look. Mushrooms and pods come attached to stems, wires or wood picks, making them easy to use.

hairy pod

sponge mushroom

lotus pod

bell cup pod

mehogni pod

giant acorn

Cones

Different types of cones are available for purchase, many with heavy stems attached (some have even been cut apart to resemble flowers!) Or you can collect your own cones to use in projects.

Always use fresh cones; if they crumble in your hands, they are too old. Rinse them under running water to remove dust and debris, then bake on a cookie sheet at 225° for one hour to open the petals again. Cones can be glued, wired or inserted directly into a project, depending on the look wanted and how they are prepared.

Mosses

Mosses are most often used to cover the mechanics of an arrangement, such as foam, wire or glue. The moss in a design is chosen for its color or texture and is secured with U-shaped floral pins or glue.

Natural Spanish moss is gray; if a soft, neutral look is desired, it works nicely. A product called gray American Moss® imitates Spanish moss but is actually excelsior; it's cleaner to use, with nearly the same effect. Other colors are available in American Moss®, such as green and brown, which can be useful when you want it to be part of the design.

Sphagnum moss, also known as sheet moss, is used when a green "growing" look is needed. It comes packaged in layers or in sheets to be peeled apart as needed.

Reindeer moss is gray with a unique texture that looks great when it can be seen as part of the design. It's available dried or preserved; dried moss is very brittle, whereas the preserved moss is softer.

Ming moss is light gray, also with an interesting texture, and looks very much like tiny plants. It's available in solid pieces which are broken apart for use. It looks nice either used as part of the design or just to cover mechanics.

Mood moss is a very thick green moss and is effectively used in designs where the moss is visible as an important component. It has depth, is firm and is easy to work with, especially on larger projects.

Tools, Supplies & Putting It All Together

The following pages include explanations and photos of all kinds of floral tools and supplies. Sometimes it's difficult to know just which supplies are really needed to complete a project; this information should clear up some of the confusion and make it easier to decide what you need and when you need it. There are some tips for using certain supplies, too.

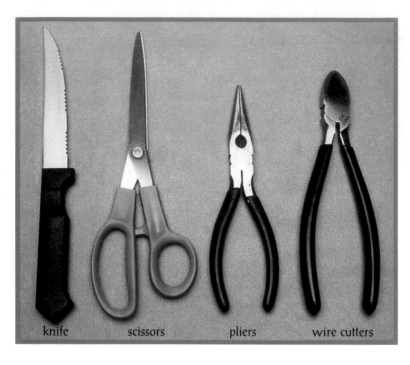

Tools

A sharp serrated knife, scissors, needle-nose pliers, and heavy-duty wire cutters are valuable tools in dried and silk floral work. The wire cutters need to be sturdy enough to cut through the heavy stems of hand-wrapped silks. Use the pliers to twist wires together, saving tender hands and fingernails. The knife trims floral foam to fit a base. Scissors should be sharp enough to cut ribbons, and shouldn't be used to cut wire, which will nick and dull the blades.

knife   scissors   pliers   wire cutters

Wires

(A) Wires are measured by gauge—the smaller the number, the heavier the wire. 18–20 gauge wire is used to lengthen or strengthen flower stems (see "Floral Tape," page 14). 22–24 gauge wire is a nice weight for bows or loop hangers. 30-gauge wire is very fine and can be used to attach stems to bases and to secure ribbon loops. (B) Paddle wire is medium-weight wire rolled onto a wooden paddle and is used whenever a continuous length is needed.

(C) Cloth-covered wires come in either green or white. Green wires resemble flower stems and blend in well with designs. The white wire is useful when doing bridal work. Both are available in stem weight as well as lighter weights for securing items together.

(D) Chenille stems can be used instead of wire to secure bows. Because of their fuzziness, they don't slip as easily—and because of their wide range of colors, it's easy to match them to your ribbon.

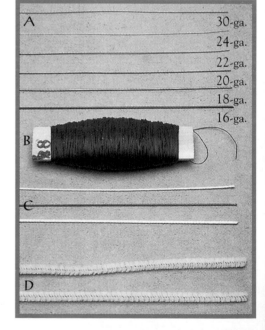

A   30-ga.
     24-ga.
     22-ga.
     20-ga.
     18-ga.
     16-ga.
B

C

D

Making a Wire Hanger

First decide the best placement for a hanger so the project hangs correctly (some projects, such as a long garland, will require more than one hanger). Insert a 6"–10" length of 20-gauge wire into the back (such as among the vines of a wreath). Bring the end back out and twist both ends together, forming a loop. If the object is solid and a wire can't be inserted, make a wire loop first and hot glue it to the back as shown at the right. (White wire was used in these photos for visibility.)

Glues

Tacky craft glue effectively secures stems in floral foam. Dip the cut stem into glue, then insert it into the project. Gluing keeps stems from twisting in or dislodging from the foam, ruining established design lines.

Hot or low temperature glue guns are handy for floral designing. The low temperature gun is safer, but not as secure as hot glue when used on items preserved with glycerine. Apply glue to the stem end, then insert it into foam or onto the base. Hold the item for a moment until the glue sets.

Glue pans, which hold a pool of melted glue at a constant temperature, are useful when you have a lot of gluing to do, since they let you keep one hand free by allowing you to dip the stems.

Floral Foam

Floral foam is available in two types: fresh or "wet" foam and dry foam. Wet foam should be used only for fresh flowers. Because it is made to soak up water and hold it for the fresh stems; it's too soft for dried and silk arrangements. Dry foam, designed to be used with silk and dried flowers, is firmer and holds stems more securely.

To prepare dry foam prior to attaching it to a base, use a serrated knife to cut it to size—trim away as much as possible, leaving a smaller area to be concealed. Cut the corners down to make it fit; if placed in a container, trim it to match the container with 1" extending above the rim. If the foam is to fit into one end of a basket, be sure to trim away enough so the foam fits snugly against the basket side.

Use the knife to round the top edges and corners of the foam. This will make it easier to cover with moss or excelsior and make the "ground" where the stems are inserted look more natural. Do not cut away so much of the foam that it no longer extends the correct amount above the rim of the container. It's much easier to achieve a natural, growing look in an arrangement if you're able to insert stems into the foam sides parallel with the table. Usually no more than 1" needs to extend above the rim to achieve this effect.

If a design requires a ball of floral foam, carve a block into a ball. It doesn't have to be perfectly round, since the flowers will cover it, but take care that the finished design is round and well-balanced.

To attach floral foam to a base, glue or wire it in place. To wire it, first cover an area on the top of the foam with a strip of moss or excelsior, then wrap a 30-gauge wire length over the foam and around the base, twisting the ends at the back to secure. The moss prevents the wire from pulling through the foam. Spread tacky glue over the top of floral foam in a container, then add a thin layer of moss. When you insert the stem through the moss into the foam, it will be glued in place.

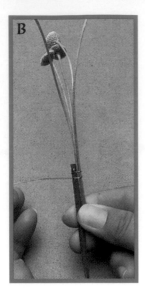

Wood Picks

These add length or strength to floral items. To add a wired wood pick to a cluster of dried flowers, (**A**) position the flowers in the cluster at varying heights, then cut the stems in the same place. (**B**) Place the stems against the pick; wrap the wire around both the pick and the stems. (**C**) Continue wrapping down the pick for 1", then wrap back up the stems, using all the wire.

Wood picks also come without wires. These can be floral-taped to stems or glued to the backs of stemless items such as pods, charms and novelties.

U-Shaped Floral Pins

Also called "greening pins," these are used to pin moss, ribbon loops, or other items into foam. If the item being secured has a tendency to spring out of the foam, apply a dab of glue to the pin ends before inserting.

For very heavy or bulky items such as plush animals, large U–pins can be made by bending 16- or 18-gauge wire.

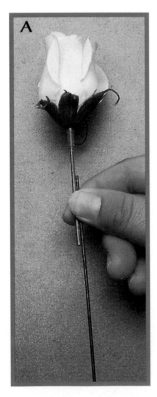

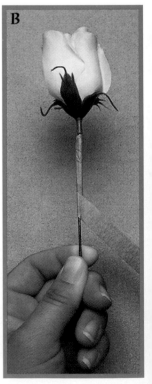

Floral Tape

This is a paper tape which has a waxy coating; stretching the tape as it's being wrapped makes it to stick to itself. Use floral tape to secure wire or a pick to a flower stem, lengthening or reinforcing it (also called "stemming a flower"). (**A**) Place a length of 18-gauge wire next to the stem of a flower.

(**B**) Wrap the stem and the wire together with floral tape, gently stretching the tape so it adheres to itself. Tape to the end of the wire.

Measuring and Cutting Floral Stems

A "stem" refers to the entire stem of flowers as purchased. When cut apart, the pieces are called "sprigs," "clusters" or "sections."

When a **blossom width** is given, measure the open flower head.

When a **blossom height** is given, measure only the blossom.

When a **stem length** is given, measure only the stem.

When a **flower length** is given, measure from the top of the blossom to the end of the stem.

Unless otherwise specified, flower measurements given within a project include 1½"–2" of stem to be inserted into the design. By cutting the stems with extra length, you are able to adjust the height of the flower within the arrangement, playing with it until it's exactly right. Using tacky craft glue to secure stems lets you, while the glue is still wet, pull out a stem that is too long, trim and reinsert it without destroying the foam. If a stem is too short, lengthen it with a stem wire (see "Floral Tape," page 14), then cut to the correct length.

Wiring a Cone

To wire a cone so it can be attached to a base: A) Use a 10" length of 24-gauge wire. Measure 3" from one end and insert the wire between two rows of cone petals near the bottom.

B) Wrap the wire around the cone, pulling tightly, then twist the wire ends so they extend from the cone. Use these wire ends to attach the cone to the project. For another look, wrap the wire among the upper petals so the bottom of the cone will show in the project.

Three Ways to Attach a Pick or Stem to a Pod or Cone

A) Drill a hole into the bottom. Fill the hole with glue and insert the blunt end of an unwired wood pick into the hole.

B) Wrap the wire of a wood pick around the cone petals, pulling it down inside the cone. Wrap completely around the cone, using all the wire.

B) Hot glue a U-shaped floral pin to the cone bottom.

RIBBONS & BOWS

Some people think one of the most difficult tasks in making a floral project is making the bow. Not so! It's true, there are stories circulating in the office about how long it took me to attempt my first bow—but once I learned, bow-making became very easy and one of the most enjoyable aspects of floral design.

My advice is to buy a reel of inexpensive acetate ribbon—enough so you don't feel guilty using as much as you want—and practice making bows. The freedom of knowing you can use as much as you want until you get it down makes learning much easier than if you use the expensive tapestry ribbon you bought just for a certain project. Eventually, making bows will become second nature (and you'll be asked by everyone in your house, office or neighborhood to please make this one bow for little Jennifer's birthday gift . . .well, you get the picture). Of course, you could offer to teach a class on bow-making to all those friends, family members and neighbors.

We've included instructions, photos and illustrations of the most popular bows. Generally, if you choose a narrower ribbon than the one suggested, you will need more of it to make sure the bow has the same impact within the design. Likewise, if a wider ribbon is chosen, you'll probably want fewer loops to make sure the bow doesn't overpower the project.

Ribbons and bows are beautiful additions to florals, but the styles of ribbons available are almost endless, and it can be confusing to choose just the right pattern for a project. However, you'll find that the flower colors and the style of the arrangement will help you narrow your choices.

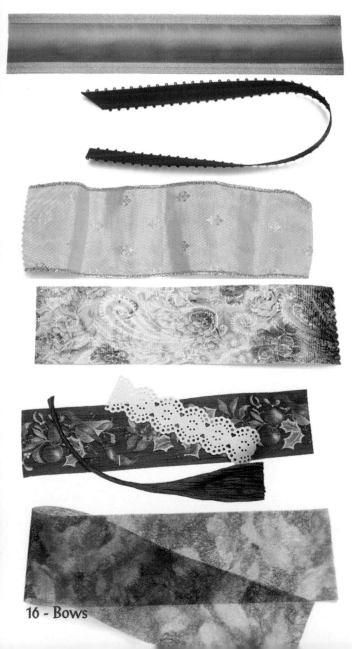

Ribbon Styles

Ribbons are available with different edge treatments; this can be important in design, as some edges will fray with frequent handling. *Woven edge ribbon* has a finished edge which will not fray. This ribbon is easy to use in bows because of its softness and pliability.

Picot ribbon is a woven edge ribbon distinguished by small loops extending outward from each edge. Including picot ribbon with plain ribbons in a multi-ribbon bow adds texture and interest. Picot ribbons add a nice touch to Victorian or romantic designs.

Wire-edged ribbon is wonderful to use because it has "memory"; each edge is woven around a thin wire. If a bow becomes crushed it's easy to reshape the loops, making the bow look new. The tails can be rippled and tucked among design components, with the wires holding the shape. The wires can be pulled to easily shirr the ribbon.

Cut edge ribbons are often used in floral work. Less expensive, they are available in many of the same patterns and designs as woven or wire-edged ribbon. To reduce fraying, sizing is added—this stiffens the ribbon, but also means that any creases made in forming the bow will remain visible. Eventually the edges will fray, so handle the ribbon as little as possible.

Paper ribbon has become a floral design staple. Some of these ribbons come twisted into cords and can be used that way, or untwisted to make crinkly flat ribbon. The twisted cords make fun accents twined through and around a bow made from flat paper ribbon. Printed paper ribbons are marketed both on reels or in packaged lengths. Their patterns are muted, making them nice for dried arrangements. Also available are lacy paper ribbons with cut-out areas resembling eyelet.

An attractive style of ribbon is made from non-woven, lightweight fabric resembling interfacing material, printed with a pattern. Because of its texture, the patterns and colors are somewhat muted. It is easy to form bows with this ribbon because it's so sheer and easy to handle.

Choosing Your Ribbons:

The ribbons you use can determine the entire look of your design. For example, heavy tapestries give a more European look, while narrow satin ribbons add a light, romantic effect. The ribbon should tie the design together and actually become part of it.

In choosing a ribbon, both color and width play important roles. Incompatible colors or textures can produce a jarring effect. Using a ribbon which has all the colors in the design—or nearly all of them—ties the design together.

If one ribbon with the right colors can't be found, use two or three ribbons, each in one of the colors needed, and stack the bows. Make a large bow of the widest ribbon (usually the dominant color in the design), then wire or glue a smaller bow of narrower ribbon to the center of it.

Another method of tying colors together is to make one bow of several different ribbons. Hold them together and handle as if they were one length to make a bow of the desired size and type.

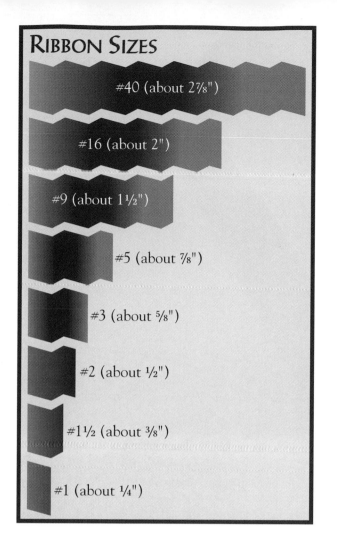

RIBBON SIZES

#40 (about 2⅞")

#16 (about 2")

#9 (about 1½")

#5 (about ⅞")

#3 (about ⅝")

#2 (about ½")

#1½ (about ⅜")

#1 (about ¼")

HOW MUCH DO I NEED?

Although projects in this book include the yardage needed for each bow in the materials list, you may want to make a different bow. First decide how many loops and tails you want, and how long they will be (if you want a center loop, double its length, add ½" and add this measurement along with the tails.) Then do this easy math:

1. ____" (loop length) x 2 + ½" extra (for the twist) = **A**

2. **A** x (number of loops) = **B**

3. **B** + ____" (tail length) + ____" (tail length) = **C**

4. **C** ÷ 36" = yardage required.

FOR EXAMPLE:

To make a bow with eight 4" loops, a 6" tail and a 7" tail,

1. 4" x 2" + ½" = **8½"**

2. 8½" x 8 loops = **68"**

3. 68" + 6" (tail length) +7" (tail length) = **81"**

4. 81" ÷ 36" = 2.25 or 2¼ yards.

Many times ribbon is used to bring different design elements together visually. This is done by rippling or looping ribbon lengths or the bow tails among the other materials in the project. Twisting the ribbon as it's looped adds interest. If the base is visible in one area of the design (such as on a vine wreath with all the flowers at the upper left), wrapping the ribbon around the bare areas will help tie the design together. The ribbon draws your eye into the undecorated space.

Other materials such as pearls, beads, or wired star garlands can be used with or in place of ribbon.

For wide ribbons a "couched" effect can be achieved by pinching the ribbon every few inches and wrapping the pinched areas with 30-gauge wire. The ribbon will puff between the wires. Glue the wired areas into the design.

Shoestring Bow

1 Measure the desired tail length from the end of the ribbon, then make a loop of the specified length. Wrap the free end of the ribbon loosely around the center of the bow.

2 Form a loop in the free end of the ribbon and push it through the center loop. Pull the loops in opposite directions to tighten, then pull on the tails to adjust the size of the loops. Trim each tail diagonally or in an inverted V.

Collar Bow

1 Form a ribbon length into a circle, crossing the ends in front. Pinch together, forming a bow, and adjust the loop size and tail length. If no tails are desired, form the length into a circle and just barely overlap the ends before pinching into a bow.

2 Wrap the center with wire and twist tightly at the back to secure. Trim the wire ends, then wrap a short length of ribbon over the center wire and glue the ends at the back. Cut each tail diagonally or in an inverted V.

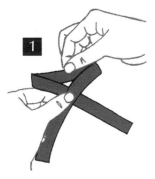

Dior Bow

1 Similar to a collar bow, this one is made with four ribbon lengths. Cut a 3", a 9", an 11", and a 12" length of ribbon. Form the 12" length into a circle.

2 Pinch in the center to make a bow shape.

3 Center the 9" and 11" lengths under the bow for tails and wire them all together at the middle. Wrap the 3" length over the wire and glue the ends at the back. Cut each tail diagonally or in an inverted V.

Flat Bow

1 Begin with one end of the ribbon and make a center loop the desired length. Twist the ribbon to keep the right side showing.

2 Make a loop the specified length on one side of your thumb. Twist the ribbon and form a matching loop on the other side.

3 Continue making loops of graduating sizes on each side of your thumb, positioning each just under the last loop, until the desired number is reached. For the tails, bring the ribbon end up and hold in place under the bow.

4 Insert a wire length through the center loop. Bring the ends to the back, catching the ribbon end, and twist to secure. Cut the ribbon tails to the desired lengths, then trim each tail diagonally or in an inverted V.

Oblong Bow

1 Form a center loop by wrapping the ribbon around your thumb. Twist the ribbon a half turn to keep the right side showing, then make a loop on one side of the center loop.

2 Make another half twist and another loop on the other side. Make another half twist and form a slightly longer loop on each side of your hand; notice these loops are placed diagonally to the first loops.

3 Make two more twists and loops on the opposite diagonal. Continue for the desired number of loops, making each set slightly longer than the previous set.

4 **For tails:** Bring the ribbon end up and hold in place under the bow. Insert a wire through the center loop, bring the ends to the back of the bow, and twist tightly to secure. Trim each tail diagonally or in an inverted V.

Puffy Bow

1 If a center loop is required, begin with one end of the ribbon length and make the center loop. Twist the ribbon to keep the right side showing. If no center loop is called for, begin with step 2.

2 Make a loop on one side of your thumb. Give the ribbon a twist and make another loop on the other side of your thumb. Continue making loops and twists until the desired number is reached (a ten-loop bow has five loops on each side), ending with a twist.

3 **For tails:** Follow step 4 of the Oblong Bow, above.

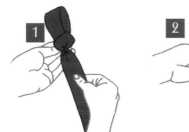

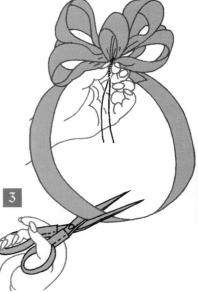

Loopy Bow

1 Measure the desired tail length from the end of the ribbon and make a loop on each side of your thumb. If a center loop is needed, measure the desired tail length from the end of the ribbon and make the center loop before the bow loops.

2 Continue making loops on each side of your thumb until the desired number is reached (for a ten-loop bow, make five loops on each side).

3 Wrap the center with wire and twist tightly at the back to secure. If a center loop was made, insert the wire through it before twisting the ends at the back. Trim the wire ends. Cut each tail diagonally.

4 Another method of securing the bow is to wrap a length of ribbon or cord around the center and tie it at the back—this also adds a second set of tails.

Loopy Bow
with Center
Loop

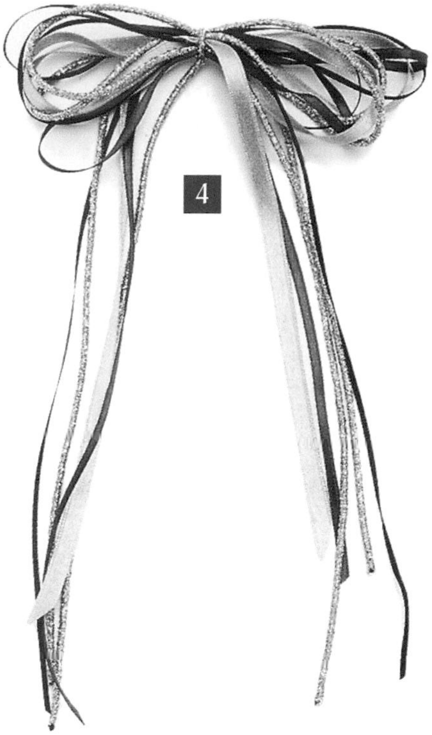

Standup Bow

1 Measure the desired tail length and hold the ribbon. Make a loop, positioning it to extend upward beside the tail.

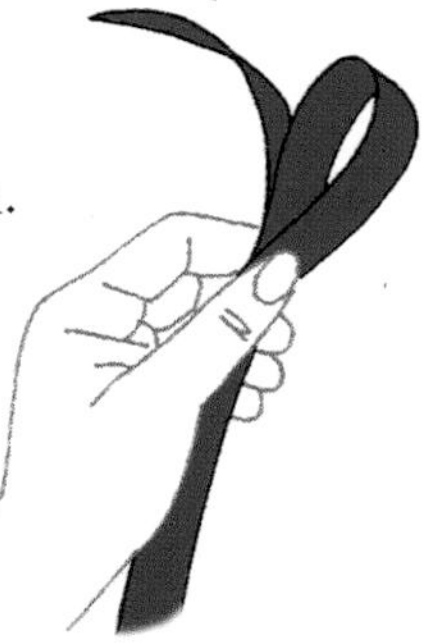

2 Repeat to make as many loops as desired. Fold a tail up to match the first tail, then trim the ribbon. Wrap wire tightly around the bottom of the loops to secure.

Ribbon Loops

1 Beginning at one end of the ribbon, make a loop of the specified size. Fold the tail back to extend beyond the end of the loop; pinch and wire the loop to a wood pick.

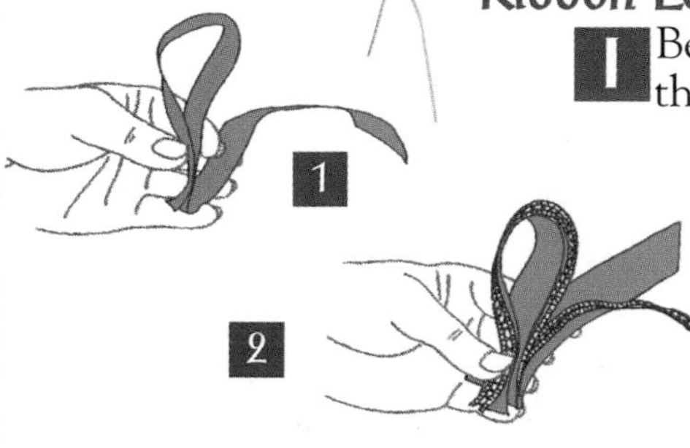

2 To add other materials to the loops, hold them over the ribbon while the loop is being made. Raffia, narrow ribbons, lace, and cord are all materials which can be effectively added to ribbon loops. For a different look, omit the tail.

CHOOSING FLOWERS

Flowers used for floral design are classified according to their function in an arrangement. To achieve a spectacular look, it is important to choose flowers which complement each other. Consider colors, textures, sizes, and shapes of flowers and materials which will go into the design.

Fluff silk flower, pine or fir stems before using in a project. Garlands are usually sold coiled, so the sprigs are all mashed close to the main stem. Bend the stems and sprigs to curve naturally. If the leaves are wired, shape them to extend among the blossoms or fruit. On pine or fir wreaths, shape each sprig to extend as desired; usually angling them all one

direction, either clockwise or counter-clockwise around the wreath, provides the most natural look to the wreath. Grape stems usually have wired tendrils which may be stretched out of shape. Wrap the tendrils around a round pen; remove the pen and slightly stretch the coil for a natural look.

Mass flowers are heavy blossoms—or they may be clusters of smaller blossoms, such as hydrangeas. They fill large areas and usually are the focus of the design, just because their mass draws the eye. Groups of small flowers such as daisies function as mass flowers when they are perceived as a unit.

Line flowers are long, narrow flowers or materials, such as snapdragons, wheat or even bare twigs. Line materials pull your eye through the design, letting you "discover" the elements. Make sure line flowers lead the eye *through* the design, rather than *out* of it.

Filler flowers are small, airy materials which fill space within a design. They become a background for the focal flowers and fill any empty areas which might otherwise disrupt the viewer's discovery trail through the design.

Textures: Many different textures are available in silk and dried flowers. Putting too many similar textures together can be boring. Mums have a busy texture and are complemented by a smooth-textured flower such as a small lily or something with few petals. Smooth berries make a nice counterpoint to a very textured carnation.

Sizes: Varying the sizes of the flowers used in a design is important to maintain interest. If all are the same size, it is difficult to understand where to look first. Generally, large mass flowers become the focal point, medium-sized flowers are added for interest and to fill out the design, then small filler flowers are inserted to fill empty areas.

Shapes: Flower shapes play a very important role in design. Just as you wouldn't want flowers all the same size or all the exact same color, you don't want flowers all the same shape in an arrangement. Elongated flowers or branches of flowers become the strong line in a design and lead your eye through the arrangement. Mixing "line" flowers with round or "mass" flowers adds interest to the design. Small "filler" flowers do just that, filling empty spaces within the design.

COLOR

Color is usually the first element of a design to which people react. It can make or break a floral design! Knowledge of a color wheel can be very helpful in deciding which colors to use together. Silk flowers come in many different hues, tints, tones and shades of color. *Hue* is the full intensity of a color; *tint* is the color with white added, *tone* is the color with gray added, and *shade* is the color with black added.

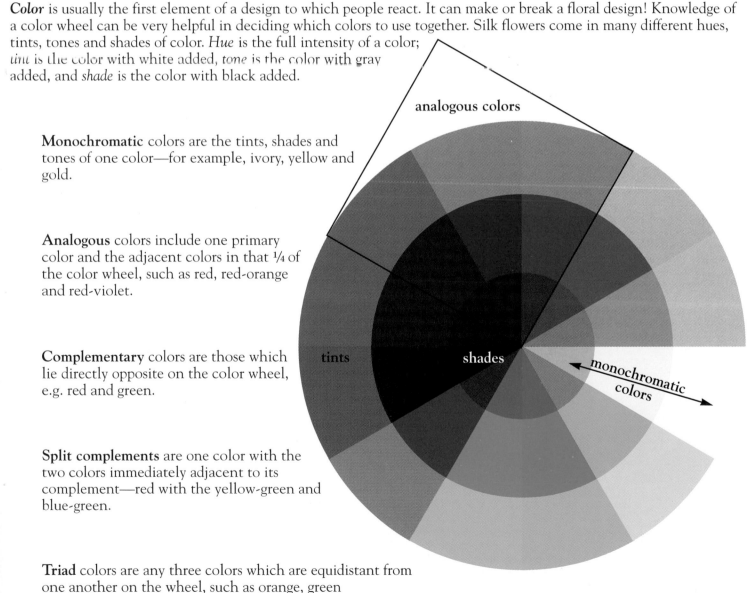

Monochromatic colors are the tints, shades and tones of one color—for example, ivory, yellow and gold.

Analogous colors include one primary color and the adjacent colors in that ¼ of the color wheel, such as red, red-orange and red-violet.

Complementary colors are those which lie directly opposite on the color wheel, e.g. red and green.

Split complements are one color with the two colors immediately adjacent to its complement—red with the yellow-green and blue-green.

Triad colors are any three colors which are equidistant from one another on the wheel, such as orange, green and purple.

DESIGN STYLES

The shape of a design depends on the type of flowers used and the container or base shape. It may be symmetrical or asymmetrical, but the elements of the design should be balanced. If an item of a certain mass or scale is used in one area of the design, it must have a balancing counterpart in the opposing area. In the wreath at right, note the red liatris flowers, one on each side of the wreath. Although they are not placed symmetrically, they are in balance.

page 114

VERTICAL:
The entire design is very narrow and tall. The materials pull the eye up or down through the arrangement, with varying textures and colors providing interest.

page 74

HORIZONTAL:
All the materials extend between two horizontal lines. Again, the diversity of materials provides the interest.

page 139

page 115

CIRCULAR:
The components are kept within a circular outline—in this case, they follow the shape of a round wreath base. A rounded centerpiece in which all elements radiate from a central point is another example of the circular style.

page 55

OVAL:
The components are kept within an oval outline—in this case, a very elongated oval.

CRESCENT:

The components are arranged to follow a smooth curve. Generally they stay within the crescent, but they may be intersected by other materials, bringing the viewer's eye back into the center of the design.

page 104

page 72

SYMMETRICAL TRIANGLE:

A vertical center line divides two halves which are roughly equal in shape and size. It's not necessary for the two sides to be mirror images, or even to contain the same materials, but they must be visually equal and balanced.

ASYMMETRICAL TRIANGLE:

The vertical line of the triangle is off-center, perhaps even along one side of the design, so that one side is visually heavier than the other.

page 73

page 60

HOGARTH CURVE:

A very graceful line is established along a relaxed S-curve. Silk flowers are easily manipulated and shaped to this line.

SUBSTITUTING FLOWERS

It's an easy task to substitute other flowers for ones listed in a project. If colors need to be changed to match your decor, determine the dominant color in the design and buy the number of flowers listed in the desired color. Repeat through the list, substituting your chosen colors for the ones listed. When you've gathered all the flowers, hold them together in a bunch to make sure you like the way the new colors blend or contrast with each other.

If one flower in a design is unavailable in your store, look around to find one similar to it. Check to make sure it's approximately the same size and that there are as many blossoms as needed. If you're substituting a different type flower, make sure it's the same shape: A 3" wide rose or carnation might be substituted for a 3" wide mum. The texture will be a little different but the design shouldn't suffer for it.

Many times it may be difficult to find just the exact Christmas pick described in the text of a project. In this case, the colors and "look" of the pick used become more important than what exactly is in it. If the project is to be woodsy or have a natural look, then the pick needs to have that same look and have the desired colors. If the project is a wreath with a red Santa on it, then picks with red presents would be appropriate; if it's a St. Nicholas in burgundy, then picks containing burgundy poinsettias would work very well.

Substituting dried materials when the correct type can't be found isn't difficult either. If you're looking for a certain cone or pod, any cone or a pod of similar size and color could be used instead. If several styles of pods are needed to complete a project, it's probably important that different pods are used, but maybe not those exact ones. (If all the same kind were used, the design might become boring; different styles of pods add texture and interest to a piece.)

If a certain dried flower or grass is unavailable, look at that material in the photo and try to find one which is similar. For instance, fillers such as gypsophila, rice grass, baby's breath and caspia can easily substitute for each other because they have similar characteristics, with fine flowers or seeds which will extend equally well among the larger components of the arrangement. If the product is bulky or heavy, then substitute a a product of similar weight. Or, if you're adventurous, try adding an unusual or different product for a completely new look.

Many times silk flowers can substitute for dried ones, too. Silk baby's breath comes in different colors and is easy to add into an arrangement which originally calls for dried baby's breath. There are many latex fruits, pods and vegetables which are great substitutes for similar dried materials. The advantage to using silk and latex pieces in place of dried materials is their longevity. They don't shatter like dried materials, allowing the arrangement to remain beautiful for a longer period of time. Dried materials lend a realistic touch to the arrangements, adding texture and natural colors, but that can be achieved with silk substitutions as well.

It's a little more difficult to substitute dried flowers for silk. Generally, air-dried blossoms are smaller, thus harder to use as a large focal point in a design. Not every polysilk is available as a dried flower, so substituting other flower types may be necessary when converting a silk arrangement to drieds.

DRYING YOUR OWN FLOWERS

To harvest flowers and foliage, cut them in the afternoon of a dry day. Flowers should be picked before they reach their prime (roses should be picked just before the buds open).

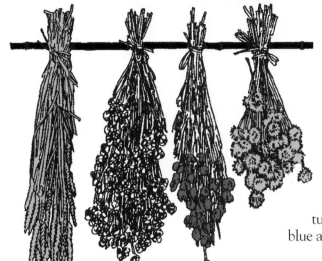

Air drying is the easiest preserving method. Remove the lower leaves and use a soft cloth to dry the entire flower. Tie several stems together, separating the flower heads as much as possible to allow air around them. Suspend the bunch upside down in a dry, dark room. Check them periodically; humidity will determine how quickly the flowers dry. Some materials, such as baby's breath, hydrangea, grains and seed heads, can be dried upright. Leaves, cones and mosses dry best lying flat.

Silica gel can also be used for preserving flowers. It draws the moisture from the plant while in its natural position so the dried flower more closely resembles its fresh self. Silica gel crystals must be moisture-free before using. If the gel is pink, it contains water. Follow the manufacturer's directions to dry it by baking. Let it cool in the oven until it is deep blue and completely dry before using.

Cut the flower stem to 1". Because plants dried with desiccants like silica gel become very brittle, it is best to attach a wire stem before drying. Use a 1½" length of 20-gauge wire and follow the directions in "Floral Tape" on page 14. Spread ½" of silica gel in the bottom of an airtight container. Place the flowers upright in the silica. Carefully pour in more silica, making sure it surrounds all flower parts but does not distort the shape. Completely cover the flowers and seal the container. Check after 48 hours. Don't leave the flowers in the crystals longer than necessary, as they can become brittle. When they are dry, carefully pour off the silica and use a soft paintbrush to remove crystals from the flower petals.

A **microwave oven** can be used with silica gel to dry flowers—do not add wire stems to these flowers. Use a microwave-safe container with a lid and fill as in the previous paragraph. Process with 300–350 watts of power. Exact cooking times will vary because of differences in ovens and plant moisture; several blooms in a half pound of silica will take 2–3 minutes. After baking, allow the flowers to stand in the silica until it is cool (10–15 minutes). Remove the flowers as described above; if they are not dry enough, microwave again.

Glycerine is another option for preserving plants such as fresh baby's breath, gypsophila, eucalyptus, ferns, evergreens and leaves. Mix equal parts glycerine and nearly boiling water. Remove any lower leaves and cut the stems at an angle. Pound the lower stems of woody plants with a hammer so they will absorb the glycerine better. Place the stems in a jar with 4" of the solution—single leaves can be soaked in a bowl. Place in a cool, dark room for 6–10 days, checking occasionally. When small beads of glycerine form on the upper ends of the plants, enough has been absorbed. If too much glycerine is absorbed, the plant will become limp. Remove the plant and wash it in soapy water, then pat dry.

COLORING FLORALS

Painting is the simplest method of coloring plant materials. There are spray paints made especially for this purpose which are very effective and come in a wide color range; be sure to use them outside. Begin with a very light misting of paint, holding the flower 1"–2" away from the nozzle. Let dry; repeat until the desired coverage is attained. Lightly spraying several shades of a color onto a flower produces a more natural look.

Dye dried flowers by adding a floral dye to the glycerine solution. Leaves can fade during the preserving process; a strong green dye will keep them deep green, or add dark red or rust dye to produce an autumnal appearance.

Sometimes a touch of sparkle adds vibrance. Spray glitter is an effective tool which comes in a variety of colors. Many Christmas designs benefit nicely from a light coat of gold or silver. Working outdoors, hold the can about 8" from the surface; spray lightly. Add more as desired.

Wrapped Up In Wreaths

One of the most popular floral bases is the wreath. It comes in all shapes, sizes and materials and can be used hanging or sitting—even broken apart for pieces to use in other designs. In this book, I've used every type of wreath from the basic straw to the more unusual root wreath. While straw and grapevine are the most common wreath types found in craft stores, there are twig, pine cone, lacquered and bleached vine wreaths as well.

In choosing a wreath as a base consider the final look desired. Bleached vines are very light and are great in garden-style designs; they also look wonderful hung on a medium-tone textured wall. Lacquered grapevines create an upscale, more elegant look and work well with magnolias, cabbage roses or gold-brushed latex fruit and tapestry ribbons.

Often unusual materials in the wreath dictate how to design the piece. If the vines or roots are pretty, interesting, and full of texture it's better to only partially decorate the wreath, allowing those vines to become an important part of the design. If the wreath is a sunburst with twigs radiating out from the center, keep the decoration fairly simple so it doesn't compete with the base and make the design too confusing.

The wreath shape also indicates what lines the design can follow. Heart-shaped, oval and teardrop wreaths have been used in this book, as well as the usual round shapes. An unusual shape may provide a finished piece which fits your wall space better than a round wreath does.

While a round wreath can be decorated with a crescent-shaped design, rather than completely covered, the placement of materials determines the success of that design. A crescent on a wreath can be fun in that it can be located almost anywhere on the base. While the upper left or right area of a wreath is usually, to me, the most interesting placement, maybe centering the design on the bottom works better with the particular materials I've chosen. For example, if the flowers are heavy or large placing them on the bottom often looks better.

Different looks can also be achieved by varying the amount of material used in each design. A full, opulent, rich feeling is achieved with an abundance of materials. However, make sure they are correctly positioned to ensure a pleasing look.

Don't stack them on top of each other, creating a crowded feeling. Instead fill the front, inner and outer edges of the wreath with the materials so they appear to "grow" evenly at the correct angles.

Maybe a lighter, sparser feeling is desired for a natural and woodsy look. Again the materials should be placed to create a balanced and harmonious piece, even though fewer components will be used. If a large or heavy piece is used, make sure it's balanced within the design, either by placing it as the focal point or adding a similar-sized component opposite it.

And don't be afraid to cut a wreath apart! Many times that's when it becomes most interesting to view, as it becomes something more than a round base—and less restricting with which to design. Or maybe you want a looser, less formal look in a grapevine wreath. In that case, cut the binding wires or vines off the wreath and pull the circular vines apart to the desired shape and placement. Wire them to each other to secure the shape, then produce a unique design—something no one else has!

Spring Birdhouse Wreath

two 10" wide bleached grapevine
  wreaths
4"x4½"x2½" wood cottage-style birdhouse with a jute hanger
two 2" long green/brown mushroom
  birds
2 stems of magenta silk sweet peas, each
  with eight 2" long blossoms, 9 buds
  and many leaves
1 stem of cream/magenta silk field blossoms with three 10"–13" sprigs of
  eight 1½" wide blossoms and 2 leaves
2 oz. of naturally colored dried silene
  grass
2 oz. of green preserved sprengeri
30-gauge wire
green sheet moss
glue gun and sticks or tacky craft glue

1 Lay one wreath horizontally and prop the other ver-
tically inside it. Wire together securely on each side.
Untie one end of the birdhouse hanger. Wrap it over the
vertical wreath and retie it to the house so the house sits
inside. Glue in place angled slightly to the right.

2 Cut one stem of sweet peas to 16". Shape it to follow
the curve of the vertical wreath; wire it to extend
from under the house up the left side to the center top.
Cut the other stem into three 9" sprigs. Wire one to
extend from the center bottom of the vertical wreath up
the right side. Wire the last two to extend over the left
side of the horizontal wreath, beginning where the two
wreaths are joined.

3 Cut the field flower stem into a 6", a 7" and a 13"
sprig. Glue the 13" sprig to extend up the left side of
the vertical wreath among the sweet peas. Glue the 6"
sprig to extend up the right side and the 7" sprig at the
lower left curving forward and right over the horizontal
wreath.

4 Cut the sprengeri into 6"–12" sprigs. Glue evenly
spaced among all the materials at the same angles,
with some extending from under the house. Cut the
silene into 4"–12" sprigs and glue as for the sprengeri.
Glue ¾"–1" wide moss tufts randomly over the wreaths to
cover exposed wires and glue; add more to the back as
needed. Glue a ½" moss tuft to the house top with a bird
on it. Glue another ½" tuft to the right front of the horizontal wreath with the second bird on it. Glue two 2"
sprengeri and two 1½" silene sprigs around this bird as
shown in the large photo above.

Crocheted Wreath

ecru crocheted wreaths: one 9" wide, one 12"
    wide
1½ yards of ½" wide cream satin picot ribbon
1½ yards of ⅛" wide dark green satin ribbon
2 yards of ¼" wide dark pink satin ribbon
4 stems of pink fabric flowers, each with a 2"
    wide blossom and 6 leaves
2 stems of white silk stephanotis, each with an
    8" and an 11" sprig of 1½" tall blossoms
    and many 1½" leaves
1 oz. of naturally colored dried brisa media
    (quaking grass)
3 oz. of pink dried ti tree branches
30-gauge wire
glue gun and sticks or tacky craft glue

1 Position the small wreath over the large one, overlapping them at the center bottom; glue securely. Cut the stephanotis stems to 11". Shape one to follow the curve of the left wreath and wire in place with the stem end at the center bottom. Repeat with the other stem on the right.

2 Cut two rose stems to 9". Shape one for the left side of the wreath and one for the right; wire both in place over the stephanotis. Cut two rose stems to 5"; shape and wire one over each 9" rose stem.

3 Cut an 18" pink ribbon length and set aside. Hold all the remaining ribbons together and handle as one. Make a loopy bow (see page 21) with six 2½" loops of each color and 6"–9" tails. Wrap the center with the 18" length and knot to secure. Glue the bow over the stems at the center bottom.

4 Cut the ti tree into 3"–7" sprigs and the brisa media into 4"–8" sprigs. Glue shorter sprigs around the bow and longer ones evenly among the flowers, extending in similar directions. Attach a wire hanger to the back (see page 12). (Optional: Satin ribbon can be woven through the holes at the center of one or both of the wreaths to add more color if desired.)

Wreaths · 33

Lavender, Delphinium & Twigs

27" wide TWIGS™ sunburst wreath with a 14" opening

2 yards of 1½" wide navy satin wire-edged ribbon

3 stems of blue silk delphinium, each with an 18" section of ½"–2" wide blossoms

2 stems of green latex grape leaves, each with a 20" section of 1½"–2¼" wide leaves

2 oz. of naturally colored dried lavender

3 oz. of naturally colored dried silver king

30-gauge wire

glue gun and sticks or tacky craft glue

1 Turn the wreath over and cut away 20–25 twigs evenly spaced from the back (don't make any holes in the design of the wreath, though). Set the twigs aside for step 4. Cut the grape leaf stems to 21". Shape the leaves naturally and bend the stem to follow the inner wreath . Wire as shown.

2 Cut each delphinium stem to 18" and curve to follow the inner wreath edge. Wire them to the edge following the directions of the twigs. Bend the tips and grape tendrils to angle out toward the twigs.

3 Hide one end of the ribbon among the flowers; glue in place. Loop the ribbon among the flowers and glue to secure, angling the loops back and forth around the wreath. Trim excess ribbon; glue the end near the beginning. Attach a wire loop hanger to the upper back (see page 12).

4 Cut half the lavender into 4"–5" sprigs and glue evenly spaced among the flowers and grape leaves, angling to the inside and forward. Cut the rest into 7"–8" sprigs and glue among the flowers angled outward among the twigs. Repeat with the silver king. Cut the twigs from step 1 to 5"–6" and glue evenly spaced among the flowers and leaves, angled forward and slightly inward.

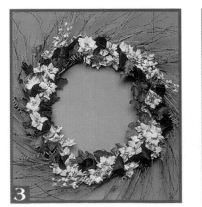

Double Wreath with Birds

grapevine wreaths: one 24" and one 10" wide
8 yards of pink Satin Twist™ ribbon
two 4" long blue/pink mushroom birds
3 stems of pink silk hydrangeas, each with a 7" wide
    head of blossoms and 4 leaves
2 stems of pink silk heather, each with fifteen 1½"
    wide clusters of pellet-like blossoms and many
    leaves
3 oz. of blue dried larkspur
8 stems of dark green preserved maidenhair fern
½ oz. of Spanish moss
30-gauge wire
glue gun and sticks or tacky craft glue

1 Securely wire the small wreath inside the upper right of the large wreath. Untwist the ribbon. Beginning at the wired area, glue one end at the back. Wrap it spiral-fashion around the large wreath; when you reach the beginning point continue to wrap around the small wreath. Trim excess and glue the end to the back.

2 Cut two hydrangea stems to 13". Overlap the stems 3" and wire them at the upper right to extend in opposite directions from the wired area of the large wreath. Cut the last hydrangea blossom head into four equal clusters. Glue one 4" from the upper hydrangea head and another 3" from that. Glue a third 4" below the right hydrangea. Glue any remaining hydrangea leaves extending from under the large and small blossoms, following similar angles.

3 Use the remaining ribbon to make an oblong bow (see page 20) with a center loop, eight 2½"–4" loops and 6" tails. Glue over the stems at the upper right. Cut the individual blossoms off the last hydrangea cluster; glue half into the center bottom of the small wreath, then glue a bird over them. Glue the remaining blossoms and bird at the center bottom of the large wreath. Cut a heather stem into a 10" and a 12" sprig. Glue angled among the upper hydrangeas; repeat with the other stem among the lower hydrangeas.

4 Cut the fern into 8"–12" sprigs. Glue them evenly spaced among all the materials. Repeat with the larkspur. Cut 2"–4" sprigs of each and glue around the birds. Attach a wire loop hanger to the upper back (see page 12).

Hydrangeas in a Heart

18" wide TWIGS™ heart wreath with a trellis back
5 yards of 2¾" wide green shimmering taffeta wire-edged
  ribbon
1 oz. of naturally colored raffia
4 stems of green/yellow fabric hydrangeas, each with a 5"
  wide blossom head and 3 leaves
3 stems of peach latex cranberries, each with 4 sprigs of five
  ⅝" wide berries and 2 leaves
2 stems of cream/yellow silk tweedia, each with 4 sprigs of
  six 1½" wide blossoms and 2 leaves
2 oz. of light green dried rattail grass
2 oz. of dark green preserved leatherleaf fern
30-gauge wire
glue gun and sticks or tacky craft glue

each berry stem, tucking the ends under the bow loops. Cut a hydrangea blossom head into two equal clusters. Glue a cluster and a leaf among the berries above the bow, 3" beyond the first hydrangea; repeat to the right of the bow.

1 Hold two raffia strands over the ribbon and handle together to make a puffy bow (see page 20) with a center loop, six 4" loops, a 12" and a 14" tail. Repeat for another bow with a center loop, two 4" loops and 27" tails. Glue the small bow to the upper right wreath. Drape the tails across the wreath and glue in place 6" above the point. Glue the large bow over the glued tails and arrange all the tails to drape below the wreath. With your fingernail, shred the raffia loops and tails into fine strands.

2 Cut two berry stems to 13". Glue one to extend from the large bow up the left wreath side and one to extend from below the bow along the right side of the wreath. Cut two hydrangea stems to 5". Glue one over

3 Cut the last berry stem into two 8" and two 6" sprigs. Glue one of each left of the small bow to extend over the wreath top. Glue the others below the bow. Cut the last hydrangea blossom into two equal pieces; glue one on each side of the bow among the berries.

4 Cut each tweedia stem into 4"–6" sprigs of 2–4 blossoms. Glue evenly spaced among the flowers near each bow. Cut the rattail grass into 3"–5" sprigs. Glue evenly spaced among all the materials, making sure sprigs near the bows extend forward as well as to the sides. Cut the fern into 4"–7" sprigs; glue near materials of similar lengths with shorter sprigs around the bows as shown in the large photo above. Attach a wire loop hanger to the upper back (see page 12).

Oval Autumn Wreath

11"x15" oval TWIGS™ vine wreath

2¾ yards of 1½" wide rust/gold/brown fall-patterned wire-edged ribbon

2 stems of rust/orange/burgundy silk fall leaves, each with five 2¾"–3½" long leaves, 2 berry clusters and pine sprigs

1 stem of latex bittersweet with eleven ¾" burgundy, green and orange pods

1 stem of latex chile peppers with twelve 2" long burgundy and green peppers and 9 leaves

2 oz. of naturally colored dried nicandra

4 oz. (4–5 stems) of naturally colored dried sabulosum cones with 1"–2" long cones on branches

30-gauge wire

glue gun and sticks or tacky craft glue

1 Cut one leaf stem to 12". Shape it to follow the curve of the wreath, then wire it extending over the wreath top from the upper right. Cut the other leaf stem to 11". Shape and wire to extend from the upper right down the right side.

2 Cut the upper 11" off the peppers and wire over the 12" leaf stem. Cut the remainder to 9" and wire over the 11" leaf stem. Shape the sprigs to extend naturally among the leaves. Cut the upper 9" off the bittersweet branch and wire over the 12" leaf stem. Cut the remainder of the bittersweet to 8" and wire over the 11" leaf stem. Shape the pods to extend naturally among the leaves and peppers.

3 Use the ribbon to make an oblong bow (see page 20) with a center loop, eight 2¼"–3¼" loops, an 18" and a 15" tail. Knot each tail 2" from the end, then glue the bow over the stems at the upper right with the long tail angled left. Loop and tuck a tail among the materials on each side of the bow, gluing as needed to secure.

4 Cut one 2" sabulosum cone off the stem and glue under the bow angled toward the wreath center. Cut the rest into 4"–5" sprigs and glue among the leaves, pods and bow loops, following similar angles. Cut the nicandra into 3"–6" sprigs and glue evenly spaced among the materials with shorter sprigs around the bow. Attach a wire loop hanger to the upper back (see page 12).

Peony & Cedar Wreath

18" wide open-weave vine wreath
3 ¼ yards of 2⅝"
wide tan/green/
burgundy printed
hopsack (roughly
woven) ribbon
2 stems of cream silk
peonies, each with
a 5" wide blos-
som, a 1½" wide
bud and 3 triple
leaf sprigs
3 stems of red latex
grapes, each with
a 6" and a 10"
sprig of ⅜"–⅝"
wide grapes, many
leaves and
tendrils
6 oz. of green
preserved cedar
3 oz. of naturally
colored dried brisa
maxima grass
(quaking grass)
30-gauge wire
glue gun and sticks
or tacky craft glue

1 Cut two 11" cedar branches. Wire them end to end at the upper left of the wreath, over-lapping the stems 2". Cut two grape stems to 12"; shape the leaves naturally and curl each tendril around your finger. Wire one over each cedar branch.

2 Cut one large peony with an 8" stem; wire over one grape stem. Repeat with the other peony, overlapping the stems 2". Cut each peony bud with an 8" stem; wire one to extend 4" beyond each large blossom. Glue any leftover leaves between the blossoms and buds.

3 Use the ribbon to make an oblong bow (see page 20) with a center loop, two 4" loops, four 5½" loops and 20" tails. Glue to the wreath between the large blossoms at the upper left. Drape the tails across the wreath to the lower right; wire them together at the point where they will be glued, then glue to secure.

4 Cut 7"–10" cedar sprigs and branches. Glue them evenly spaced among the flowers and grapes. Glue 4"–5" sprigs around the bow, making sure some extend forward. Glue 5"–8" sprigs at the lower right over the glued ribbon tails, extending along the wreath curve. Cut the last grape stem into two 7" sprigs. Glue one extending toward each side; glue any leftover leaves among the sprigs, making sure any glue and stems are covered. Glue 3" cedar sprigs into the center of the arrangement at the lower right, extending forward. Cut the grass into 4"–8" sprigs. Glue them evenly among all the materials at the upper left and lower right. Attach a wire hanger to the top back (see page 12).

Pine Cone & Fall Leaves Centerpiece

15" wide pine cone wreath
two 2" tall wood candle cups
one 7" tall wood candlestick
cream taper candles: two 12", one 10"
nine 48" long naturally colored raffia strands
one 5"x4" dried mushroom on a pick
1 orange/green silk oak bush with four 9"–10"
   branches of sixteen 3" long leaves and 3
   dried seed pods
1 stem of green latex grape ivy with three
   8"–10" sprigs of 1½"–3" long leaves and
   curled tendrils
1 stem of silk blackberries with four 4"–8" sprigs
   of ⅝" wide berries and 1½"–2" long leaves
2 oz. of naturally colored dried lino grass
2 oz. of green sheet moss
3"x3"x2" block of floral foam for silks
U-shaped floral pins, wire cutters
five 2½" long wired wood picks
glue gun and sticks or tacky craft glue

1 Use the wire cutters to pry up and remove two cones from the middle row of the wreath, leaving four cones in place between the holes. Glue a candle cup into each hole. Trim the bottom of the foam to fit over the cones centered between the candle cups; glue in place. Trim the mushroom pick to 2" long, dip in glue and insert into the back of the foam, angled toward the left.

2 Place the candlestick next to the foam inside the wreath as you're working to make sure space is left for it. Cut the branches off the oak bush. Cut two branches each into a 9" and a 7" sprig. Cut each remaining branch into four 6" sprigs. Insert a 9" sprig into each side of the foam to extend over a candle cup.

3 Insert the 7" sprigs into the center top foam, one angled inside and one to the outside of the wreath. Insert the 6" sprigs evenly spaced around the foam and on each side of the candlestick.

4 Cut the grape ivy stem into one 8" and two 10" sprigs. Insert a 10" sprig into each side of the foam beside a 9" oak sprig. Insert the 8" sprig into the back foam curving over the mushroom. Cut the blackberry into one 4", one 6" and two 8" sprigs. Insert an 8" sprig behind each 10" grape ivy sprig to curve behind the candle cup. Insert the 6" sprig into the foam center and the 4" sprig into the foam just behind the candlestick. Cut the lino grass into 4"–10" sprigs. Insert sparingly into the foam near materials of similar lengths as shown in the large photo above. Insert a candle into each cup and candlestick. Place the wreath and candlestick together on a table as shown.

9" wide Styrofoam® heart wreath
3⅓ yards of 1⅜" wide purple moiré ribbon
4 yards of ⅞" wide cream satin ribbon
2 yards of ⅝" wide purple diagonally-patterned
   ribbon with 2 sheer stripes
2 stems of lavender silk clover, each with three
   8"–12" sprigs of five 1" wide blossoms and
   many leaves
1 stem of golden cream silk mini-daisies with three
   11" sprigs of many ½" wide blossoms
1 oz. of naturally colored dried mustard grass
24-gauge wire
glue gun and sticks or tacky craft glue

1 Glue one end of the purple ribbon to the upper left wreath back and wrap it spiral-fashion around the wreath, overlapping the wraps to completely cover the foam. Glue the end at the back.

2 Glue one end of the cream ribbon over the purple ribbon end. Wrap it to the front, twist it one complete turn, then wrap it to the back. Continue wrapping and twisting around the wreath, positioning each wrap to slightly overlap the last. Glue the end at the back. Glue a wire loop hanger to the top back (see page 12).

3 Cut the clover sprigs off the stems and trim to 3"; save the leftover leaves. Starting at the upper left, glue three sprigs to curve over the shoulder to the heart center and two curving down the left side of the wreath. Use the ribbon to make a puffy bow (see page 20) with a center loop, eight 1½" loops, a 15" and a 16" tail. Glue the bow at the upper left over the clover stems. Loop and glue the tails to the bottom right, 1½"–2" above the point.

4 Cut three clover blossoms; glue them and one leaf over the glued area of the bow tails. Cut 3" long 2-sprig daisy sections. Glue evenly spaced among the upper clover. Glue three 3" sprigs around the lower clover. Glue any leftover clover leaves among the upper flowers to fill any empty spaces, as shown in the large photo above. Cut 3"–4" mustard grass sprigs and glue evenly spaced among the upper flowers. Glue 2" sprigs around the lower clover.

Wreath of Shells & Roses

14" wide straw wreath

14–16 naturally colored seashells of varied
   shapes and sizes from 1"–3" wide

6 oz. of brown American Moss™ excelsior

2 stems of cream/fuchsia silk roses, each with
   six 1"–2" wide blossoms, buds and many
   leaves

1 stem of white latex snowberries with five
   10"–11" sprigs of many ¼"–½" wide
   berries and many leaves

1 oz. of naturally colored dried brisa media
   grass (quaking grass)

1 oz. of green preserved isolepsis grass

2½" green wired wood picks

U-shaped floral pins

30-gauge wire

glue gun and sticks or tacky craft glue

1 Cover an 8" section of the wreath front, outer and inner sides with moss; wrap with wire to secure, twisting the ends at the back. Repeat to completely cover the wreath. Cut one rose stem to 16" and one to 11". Insert the 16" stem into the left side of the wreath with the top bud extending just beyond the outer wreath edge. Insert the 11" stem left of the first, shaping the flower sprigs to extend among those of the first stem with the lower sprigs forward.

2 Cut the two lowest sprigs off the berry stem and set aside. Cut the rest of the stem to 17" and insert between the rose stems; curve the sprigs and leaves among the roses. Cut each set-aside sprig to 8". Insert one on each side of the rose stems, angling them slightly forward and away from the roses.

3 Glue shells in front of the rose stems and "piled" into the wreath bottom, spilling over the front edge. Attach a wire loop hanger to the upper back (see page 12).

4 Hold 4–5 brisa stems together and cut to 16". Wire to a wood pick and insert at one side of the tallest rose. Repeat to make more brisa clusters, varying them in height from 4"–16". Insert evenly spaced near materials of similar heights and among the shells. Repeat with the isolepsis, cutting the upper portions of the grass blades to attach to the picks (see the large photo above).

Sprengeri & Honeysuckle Wreath

10" wire wreath form with prongs
gun and sticks or tacky craft glue
1 green silk sprengeri bush with six 10"–28" long branches of 4"–5" needle sprigs
2 stems of orange silk honeysuckle, each with three 8"–12" sprigs of 1" tall blossoms and leaves
2 oz. of green dried linum atraxa
3 oz. of naturally colored dried bupleurum
2 oz. of green preserved leatherleaf fern
glue gun and sticks or tacky craft glue

1 Cut all the branches off the sprengeri bush and lay them into the wreath form, taking care that the stems are hidden and the branches are distributed evenly around the form. Pull sprigs near a set of prongs upward, then bend the prongs over the branches, bending them toward the center wire. Carefully pull 4" sprigs from under the wires and fluff them to cover the wires. Repeat around the wreath.

2 Cut each honeysuckle stem into four 6"–8" sprigs. Glue them evenly spaced around the wreath, angling the same directions as the sprengeri. Cut any remaining leaves off the main stem and glue near the flower sprigs. Cut the leatherleaf fern into 3"–4" sprigs. Glue them evenly spaced around the wreath, pushing them well into the sprengeri to provide depth.

3 Cut the linum and bupleurum into 4"–6" sprigs. Glue evenly spaced around the wreath, positioning longer sprigs around the outside, shorter ones on the inside and front of the wreath. Be sure to fill any empty areas. Attach a wire loop hanger to the back (see page 12).

Woodsy Nest

20″ tall TWIGS™ teardrop wreath
3½″ blue mushroom bird
2 yards of 1½″ wide navy/black taffeta wire-edged ribbon
three 40″ strands of naturally colored raffia
2 stems of blue silk cornflowers, each with three 10″ sprigs of
  one 2″ wide blossom and a bud or small blossom and many
  leaves
1 stem of white silk mini-daisies with three 9″–15″ sprigs of
  many ¾″ wide blossoms and leaves
1 green silk piggyback plant with 8 branches of many 1″–2″
  long leaves
1 oz. of naturally colored dried mini poppies
1 oz. of green sheet moss
glue gun and sticks or tacky craft glue

1 Attach a wire loop hanger to the upper wreath back (see page 12); glue moss along the bottom. Cut the branches off the piggyback plant; set one aside for step 3. Cut the rest to these lengths: one 5″, one 6″, one 7″, four 8″. Glue an 8″ branch on the right side of the wreath extending to within 4″ of the center top. Continue gluing 8″ branches down the right side, overlapping the branches to cover the stems. Glue the 7″ just left of the last 8″ branch, the 6″ one left of it and the 5″ one left of the 6″ branch. Curve the 5″ and 6″ branches to the left.

2 Cut a cornflower sprig to 10″, one to 9″ and another to 8″ long. Glue among the tallest piggyback branches. Cut the other stem into individual blossom and bud sprigs, each 5″–7″ long. Glue evenly spaced among the shorter piggyback branches, with the shortest sprigs angled left and forward.

3 Cut the two lowest leaves off the remaining piggyback branch. Cut the branch to 3″ and glue it at the lower left side of the wreath. Glue the two leaves into the moss at the base of this sprig. Glue the bird onto the leaves.

4 Cut the daisy stem into a 9″, an 11″ and a 15″ sprig. Glue evenly spaced near flowers of similar lengths. Cut 5″–15″ poppy sprigs and glue evenly spaced near materials of similar lengths. Cut 3″–4″ sprigs and glue around the leaves on the left. Cut three daisies from the back of one sprig and glue around the bird. Hold a raffia strand over the ribbon and handle as one to make an oblong bow (see page 20) with a center loop, six 2½″–4″ loops and 11″ tails. Shred the raffia loops and tails with your thumbnail. Glue the bow at the bottom right, then loop and glue a tail up each side of the wreath. Knot each set of raffia tails 3″ from the ends; glue a knot on each side of the wreath.

Roses on a Trellis

24" wide round root wreath
one 13" tall TWIGS™ trellis
2 yards of 2¾" wide maroon/green shimmering taffeta wire-edged ribbon
2 stems of maroon silk & latex roses, each with a 5" and a 3" blossom, 2 buds and many leaves
2 stems of coral silk baby's breath, each with four 9"–11" sprigs of many ½" wide blossoms and buds
1 branch of green silk ivy with a 16" section of 2"–3½" long leaves, tendrils and woody-looking stems
1 stem of maroon/peach/burgundy latex cranberries with 4 sprigs of five ⅝" berries and leaves
2 oz. of green preserved plumosus
24-gauge wire
glue gun and sticks or tacky craft glue

1 Insert the trellis among the wreath roots at the lower left and glue to secure. Cut one rose to 20"; glue it to extend from behind the trellis to the wreath top. Pull the lower rose through to the front of the trellis and curve the buds forward left of the upper blossom. Cut the other rose to 15". Glue it in front of the trellis. Shape the roses around the left side of the trellis with the buds curving right over the trellis front.

2 Cut the ivy stem to 16". Glue it to extend from the trellis along the wreath bottom. Cut the cranberry stem to 14". Glue it over the ivy, extending to within 2" of the end of the stem.

3 Cut one baby's breath stem to 18". Glue it behind the trellis to extend between the rose stems on the left side. Cut the other baby's breath stem to 14". Glue it in front of the trellis, then shape the two taller sprigs to extend up the right side, curving right. Shape the two shorter sprigs to curve between the right side of the trellis and the wreath bottom.

4 Beginning at the wreath top, measure 5" from one end of the ribbon and glue it behind the rose. Tuck the ribbon down the left side of the wreath, gluing to secure. Glue it over the trellis base and any exposed stems, then continue tucking and gluing it across the wreath bottom. Allow the end to extend 3" beyond the ivy, then trim the excess. Cut the plumosus into 8"–15" sprigs. Glue longer sprigs behind the trellis to extend behind the long rose. Glue the rest evenly among all the materials, positioning the shorter sprigs around the base of the trellis. Attach a wire loop hanger to the upper back (see page 12).

Wreath with Fruit

18" wide lacquered grapevine wreath
4½" long brown/black feathered bird
44" long stem of artificial fruit with a peach, pears,
    berries, plums, pomegranates and many wired
    fabric leaves
1 green silk sprengeri bush with six 10"–28" long
    branches of 4"–5" needle sprigs
3 stems of peach latex cabbage roses, each with a
    4½" wide blossom, a bud and eleven 1½"–2"
    long leaves
3 oz. (3 stems) of naturally colored dried aristea
30-gauge wire
glue gun and sticks or tacky craft glue

1 From the wreath back, cut and pull out two 28" vines. On the front, insert one end of each into the vines at the upper left; wire in place. Allow the vines to curve over the wreath and down to the lower right, extending 4"–6" past the wreath. Again wire to secure.

2 Cut off and discard the lower 4" of the fruit stem. Fluff the fruit and leaves naturally; insert into the wreath center top. Wire to follow the curve of the wreath down the left side and off the edge near the ends of the added vines. Shape the excess to curve downward as shown. Pull the two fruit sprigs closest to the stem end to extend over the wreath top; shape the remaining fruit sprigs to space them evenly along the wreath.

3 Cut the branches off the sprengeri bush. Wire the 28" branch to the left side of the wreath, extending beyond the end of the fruit vine. Wire the 10" and 12" branches above the first, one on each side. Wire the 23" branch to extend up the left side 4" beyond the upper end of the fruit vine. Wire the 18" branch on the left side of the 23" branch. Fluff the sprigs.

4 Cut each rose stem to 12". Wire one to extend downward on the left with the rose just above where the two grapevines from step 1 join to the lower wreath. Wire the second with the rose just below where the grapevines join the upper wreath. Wire the third rose stem to the wreath with the blossom midway between the other two roses. Cut the aristea into 5"–8" sprigs and glue evenly among the materials following the same angles—make sure there are no empty spaces on the left where stems overlap. Glue the bird to the lower right as shown in the large photo above.

Floral Wall Decorations

One of the most warm and personal additions you can make when decorating a room is a floral wall piece. This section introduces many different looks to add excitement to your wall. While wreaths are still the most common and popular bases for floral wall decorations, there are many other equally attractive and interesting bases with which to design floral accents.

Twig forms are wonderful for floral designing and are widely available. They come in many shapes and sizes, plus they are easy to use; in fact, they almost design themselves! A swag with intricate loops of twigs is beautiful when silk and dried flowers and a tapestry ribbon are added.

Many of the original twig forms were made in the Philippines, but now American-made birch, winged elm and grapevine pieces can be found in craft stores. They are fun to design around and, depending on what you use to enhance them, can look rustic, wild, or even Victorian.

The arch shape is perennially popular in floral design. Creative designers are even turning arches upside down to be festoons, or hanging them by one end to make crescents. Arches come in a variety of vines and can have long, uneven ends. If an arch is unavailable, a large grapevine or rattan wreath can be cut in half, making two arches. Use heavy wire cutters or pruners, and be sure to cut the ends unevenly so they don't look like they've all been sawed off

at one spot. If the vines feel loose,
wrap each arch in several places with
wire to secure them.

Arched or straight swags made from twigs and
vines are great for establishing the lines of a spectacular addition over a door, a window, or even under a shelf.
They have special appeal when hung just under the shelf of a
mantle or on the wall above it.

Garlands are versatile bases which can be decorated and used either hanging on the wall or lying on a table. They make gorgeous accents when used to
frame the top and sides of a mirror or picture, or when displayed over a window.
Any configuration can be created just by changing the placement of the hangers.
And, with careful trimming, they can be shortened to the perfect length for any location.

Surprisingly, even hollow birch bark and birch branches can become terrific bases for wall decorations! The variety represented in this grouping of wall decorations should spark creativity in any-
one who's looking for that special accent needed on any wall.

Autumn Arch

22" wide wire arch form
2 yards of 1⅜" wide rust moiré ribbon
6' green/brown/rust silk grape ivy garland
    with 1"–3" long leaves
1 green/burgundy latex grape branch with
    two sprigs of five ⅞" wide grapes, ten-
    drils and many 3"–4" long leaves on a
    heavy green stem
1 latex apple branch with four
    burgundy/yellow 1¼"–1½" wide
    apples, many 2½"–4" long green/yel-
    low leaves on a heavy brown stem
one 7" wide dried mushroom on a pick
one 3½" long mehogni pod on a pick
one 3" long hairy pod on a pick
one 2" wide pine cone on a pick
4 oz. of 24"–36" long birch branches
2 oz. of naturally colored dried bromus
    secalinus grass
6" of 30-gauge wire (hanger)
glue gun and sticks or tacky craft glue

1 Cut the garland in half, trimming away any excess stem at the ends. Place the two lengths in the arch form. Pull the sprigs out of the way so they won't be caught under the wires.

2 Cut the grape stem to 21". Curve it to follow the arch shape and place it in the form over the ivy, extending left. Position it so the end comes to within 4" of the garland end. Cut the apple stem to 22", curve it and place in the form on the right side, again coming to within 4" of the garland end. As with the ivy, pull sprigs back so they aren't caught under the wires, then press the wires down in place. Position the sprigs down over the wires to hide them.

3 Trim the pick on the mushroom to ½" long. Glue it to the arch center, extending forward under the ivy leaves. Trim the picks on the cone and pods to 1". Glue over the mushroom as shown. Cut 6"–12" birch branches and glue evenly spaced among the materials, angling them toward the ends, with shorter branches closer to the center and longer ones nearer the ends. Cut 4"–6" sprigs and glue at the arch center, angling some forward among the pods and some upward at the back.

4 Position one end of the ribbon 2" from one end of the arch, then tuck and glue it over the arch, allowing it to pouf between tucks. Cut the grass into 6"–10" sprigs and glue evenly spaced throughout the arch at similar angles to the previous materials. Cut 4"–6" sprigs and glue among the pods and at the arch center. Attach a wire loop hanger at the center back (see page 12).

Baby's Breath Garland

86" of ⅜" wide sisal rope

5 yards of 1⅜" wide burgundy/green/fuchsia floral printed
   sheer ribbon

9 oz. of naturally colored preserved baby's breath

4 stems of mauve silk hollyhocks, each with 4 sprigs of two 2"
   wide blossoms and 4 leaves

6 stems of pink silk rosebuds, each with 5 sprigs of 3–5 buds,
   each ½" long, and leaves

1 green silk sprengeri bush with eight 11"–30" branches of
   many 3" sprigs

9 oz. of cranberry preserved heather

30-gauge wire (about 25–thirty 18" lengths)

glue gun and sticks or tacky craft glue

1 Cut the baby's breath into 3"–5" sprigs and the heather into 5"–6" sprigs. Cut a 30" sprengeri branch into 3-sprig sections. Secure one end of a wire length to one end of the rope. Hold one heather, one sprengeri and three baby's breath sprigs together extending past the rope end. Wrap the stems three times with the wire; do not cut the wire.

2 Place another heather, another sprengeri and three baby's breath sprigs with the blossoms just covering the preceding stems. Wrap with wire as before. Repeat to the end of the wire length, then secure the wire end to the rope and attach another length. At the rope center, secure the wire and trim the excess. Beginning at the other end of the rope, repeat steps 1 and 2.

3 Use the ribbon to make an oblong bow (see page 20) with a center loop, ten 2½"–5" long loops and 12" tails. Wire and glue it to the garland center. Make two more oblong bows, each with a center loop, two 3" loops and 6" tails. Wire one on each side of the garland 20" from the end.

4 Cut the hollyhocks and rosebuds into 4" sprigs. Glue the hollyhock sprigs evenly spaced to the garland, angled from the center toward the ends. Glue two leaves near each sprig. Repeat with the rosebuds, gluing a leaf sprig near each bud. Attach a wire loop hanger to the garland center and one behind each side bow (see page 12). Attach more hangers as needed so the garland hangs as desired.

Birds & a Bark House

5"x11" birchbark tube
two 3" long brown/black mushroom birds
1½ yards of 2¾" wide mauve/green/burgundy print wire-edged ribbon
2 stems of pink silk cherry blossoms, each with a 26" section of ¾"–2" wide blossoms and many leaves
3 stems of silk blackberries, each with an 11" section of many ⅝" wide berries and 2½" long leaves
2 stems of burgundy silk mini-daisies, each with a 17" section of many ¾" wide blossoms and leaves
½ oz. of Spanish moss
3"x3"x3" block of floral foam for silks
U-shaped floral pins
30-gauge wire
glue gun and sticks or tacky craft glue

1 If there isn't a hole in the bark, break one 4" from the top. Glue the foam to the left side; use a knife to trim the foam corners and sharp edges off. Cut each cherry blossom stem to 18". Insert one into the foam top; shape it to curve over the top of the bark. Insert the other into the foam bottom, shaping it to curve under the bark, forming a crescent.

2 Cut two 12" berry sprigs and insert one in front of each cherry blossom stem, shaping it in a similar curve. Pull some cherry blossom sprigs forward to intermingle among

the berry sprigs. Use the ribbon to make an oblong bow (see page 20) with a center loop, two 3½" and two 4" loops and 6" tails. Glue the bow to the foam between the upper and lower stems with the tails tucked among the stems.

3 Cut the remainder of each cherry stem into one 9" and two 4" sprigs. Insert a 9" sprig into the top and one into the bottom of the foam in front of the berry stems, following the curves. Insert two 4" sprigs on each side of the bow, with one left sprig angling down among the berries in front of and one behind the bow.

4 Cut each daisy stem into a 16" and a 10" sprig. Insert a long sprig near the longest cherry blossom sprig on the top and bottom of the design. Insert a 10" sprig to the left of the berry stems; curve all to follow the crescent shape. Cut the third berry stem into a 5" and a 10" sprig. Insert the 10" sprig into the bottom of the foam, shaping the berries to curve among the flowers. Insert the 5" sprig into the foam top just behind the bow. Glue a moss tuft to the bottom edge of the hole and glue the bird on top of it. Glue the second bird onto a berry near the bottom left edge of the bark. Glue moss to cover any exposed foam. Attach a wire loop hanger to the upper back (see page 12).

Bound Branches with Chilies

six 40" long birch branches with many twigs
3½ yards of 2⅝" wide rust/green/black tapestry wire-edged ribbon
1 stem of burgundy/orange/green latex crabapple with a 23" section of ⅝"–⅞" wide apples
    and many leaves
1 stem of burgundy/green latex bittersweet branch with a 15" section of many ⅝" pods
2 stems of peach latex Japanese apricot blossoms, each with a 17" section of ⅜"–½" buds
    and 1" wide blossoms
1 dried artichoke with a 3" tall head on a stem
1 oz. of green preserved tree fern
4 oz. of naturally colored dried chili pepper stems with 2"–4" peppers and leaves
three 16"–24" pheasant feathers
30-gauge wire
glue gun and sticks or tacky craft glue

1 Wire the birch branches together, varying the lengths and creating a sturdy base for the design. Trim the crabapple stem to 27"; wire it with the top 9"–10" from the twig ends. Shape the apple sprigs naturally among the twigs.

2 Cut the bittersweet branch to 18" and wire it below the crabapple stem with the lowest sprigs near the lowest birch twigs. Wire one apricot branch to extend 4" beyond the crabapple branch tip. Cut the other apricot branch to 20" and wire as for the bittersweet branch.

3 Trim the artichoke stem to 7" and wire to the branches where the lowest sprigs begin. Use the ribbon to make a puffy bow (see page 20) with a center loop, six 3½" loops and 36" tails. Wire and glue it to the branches left of the artichoke head. Loop and glue the tails through the branches, one above the crabapple stem and one nearer to the lowest branches.

4 Glue a feather to extend 2" beyond the apricot blossoms. Glue the shortest feather to extend from under the artichoke and the last between and below the first two. Cut 8"–10" chili pepper sprigs and glue evenly spaced among the flowers and branches. Cut single peppers and glue around the artichoke and below the bow; repeat with tree fern. Attach wire loop hangers (see page 12) to the back to hang the branch at an angle.

Beribboned Hat

12" wide cinnamay hat
3 yards of 1½" wide iris blue taffeta wire-edged ribbon
2 stems of cream fabric scabiosa, each with three 2½"
   wide blossoms and six
   3" long leaves
1 stem of lavender silk
   heather with 15 sprigs,
   each with one 1½"
   wide cluster of tiny
   pellet-like blossoms
   and two 2"–2½"
   wide leaves
1 oz. of sage green pre-
   served plumosus fern
1 oz. of naturally colored
   dried rice grass
24-gauge wire
glue gun and sticks or
   tacky craft glue

1 Attach a 3" wire loop hanger (see page 12) into the upper hat back near the crown. Cut 5"–6" fern sprigs and glue to the brim near the crown, beginning at the center bottom and extending for 8" around the brim on each side. Set aside the rest of the fern for step 4.

2 Cut each scabiosa into a 9", a 7" and a 5" blossom sprig. Glue one of each length to each side of the hat extending from the center bottom to curve around the crown.

3 Use the ribbon to make an oblong bow (see page 20) with a center loop, two 2", four 2¾" and two 3½" loops, and a 10", a 12", a 13" and a 15" tail. Glue it to the crown bottom with the loops curving toward each side. Cut 3" heather sprigs off the main stem. Glue two to extend downward from under the bow. Glue the rest evenly spaced among the flowers and fern sprigs on each side.

4 Cut the rice grass into 3"–5" sprigs. Glue evenly spaced among the florals at similar angles. Cut 3–4 fern sprigs to 8"–10"; glue them and 3–4 rice grass sprigs to extend downward from under the bow and heather at the center back. Glue the remaining fern sprigs evenly among the flowers, extending upward and forward to fill any empty spaces.

Harvest in a Swag

30" lacquered vine swag

2⅞ yards of 2" wide tan/dark mauve/green tapestry ribbon

1 stem of latex apples with four 1¼"–1⅝" burgundy and yellow apples and fourteen 3" green/yellow leaves

1 branch of dark mauve fabric magnolias with five 3"–4" wide blossoms and 5 leaves

1 branch of purple latex grapes with two 3"–5" long clusters of ½" wide grapes and eight 2"–3½" wide purple/green leaves

2 stems of artificial red berries, each with five 6"–8" sprigs of many ¼" wide berries and no leaves

2 oz. of green preserved plumosus fern

walnut glossy spray stain

30-gauge wire

glue gun and sticks or tacky craft glue

1 Carefully cut off 10" at one end of the swag and set the twigs aside for step 4. Position the remaining 20" with the bound area as the top. Spray the red berries with stain to darken them; let dry.

2 Cut the apple stem to 28". Position the end even with the upper end of the swag and wire it to extend down the swag center. Cut the magnolia branch to 18". Place the stem end even with the swag end and wire to extend down the right side of the apple stem.

3 Cut the grape branch to 14" and wire to extend down the left side of the apple stem. Fluff and shape the leaves, blossoms and fruit. Cut one berry stem to 22" and wire to extend from the swag top, positioning the sprigs evenly spaced among the other materials. Cut the other berry stem to 14" and wire near the swag top, fluffing the sprigs.

4 Use the ribbon to make a puffy bow (see page 20) with a center loop, six 4" loops, an 18" and a 28" tail. Glue to the swag top, then glue a tail down each side, tucking it down among all the materials. Cut the twigs from step 1 into 4"–8" lengths; glue short sprigs around the bow and longer ones evenly spaced throughout the arrangement to fill any empty spaces. Repeat with the fern, gluing 3"–4" sprigs behind the bow extending upward. Attach a wire loop hanger to the upper back (see page 12).

Hollyhock Swag

32" lacquered vine horizontal swag

2¼ yards of 2⅝" wide bur-
gundy/cream/green/gold
flowered satin wire-edged
ribbon

2 stems of yellow silk hollyhocks, each with a 20"
section of 1½"–3" wide
blossoms, buds and
leaves

2 stems of burgundy/green
silk rose hips, each with a
14" section of 1½" long
hips and many leaves

4 oz. of green preserved
mini oak

2 oz. of light green dried
rattail grass

30-gauge wire

glue gun and sticks or tacky
craft glue

1 From the swag back, cut away 20 twigs, 6"–8" long, and set aside for step 4. Cut each hollyhock stem to 21". Wire a hollyhock stem to the swag front extending from the center to 3" beyond the end. Repeat on the other end. Shape the stems to curve naturally.

2 Cut each rose hip stem to 16". Wire one to the left side of the swag below the hollyhock. Wire the other to the right side above the hollyhock.

3 Use the ribbon to make an oblong bow (see page 20) with a center loop, six 3"–4½" loops and two 12"

tails. Glue the bow to the swag center, angled to the upper area. Measure 7" from the bow wire down the right tail; glue this spot under the nearest hollyhock blossom on the right side.

4 Cut 9"–11" mini oak sprigs and glue among the vines and flowers toward each end of the swag. Cut 4"–5" sprigs and glue around the bow. Cut the rattail grass into 4"–11" sprigs and glue evenly spaced near materials of similar lengths. Glue the twigs from step 1 evenly spaced among all the materials at similar angles. Attach a wire loop hanger to the center back (see page 12).

Hydrangea & Cedar Broom

31" long pine broom
12" square white Battenberg fabric/lace doily
3 yards of 1½" wide burgundy satin ribbon with metallic gold
   embroidery and wired edges
1 stem of burgundy/green silk hydrangea with a 6"–7" wide head
   and 9 leaves
2 stems of white silk Queen Anne's lace, each with three 10" sprigs
   having one 1"–2½" wide heads of pellet-like blossoms and many
   1½" long leaves
2 stems of green/burgundy latex grapes, each with a 6" cluster of
   ⅜"–⅝" wide grapes and six 2"–3" long leaves
4 oz. of green preserved cedar
30-gauge wire
glue gun and sticks or tacky craft glue

1 Fold one corner of the doily down 6" and hold in place.
Wrap it around the broom, placing it with the lowest point
1½" above the broom bottom. Glue to secure, overlapping it at
the broom back. Cut the hydrangea to 8"; glue and wire it to
extend over the doily, angled down and right as shown.

2 Cut the grape stems to 8". Glue one above the hydrangea,
angled upward. Glue the other below and left of the
hydrangea, curving to the center bottom of the doily.

3 Use the ribbon to make an oblong bow (see page 20) with a
center loop, two 3" and four 3¾" loops, and 25" tails. Glue
between the hydrangea and the upper grape stem, angled
toward the upper left. Glue the left tail loosely wrapped up the
handle, trimming the excess.

4 Cut a 3" and a 4" long Queen Anne's lace sprig off one
stem, each with a 1" wide blossom head. Glue among
the upper grapes, extending upward. Cut the remaining sprig
from this stem and those from the other stem into 6"–8"
lengths. Glue among the hydrangea and lower grapes. Cut the
cedar into 6"–8" sprigs and glue evenly spaced into the lower
arrangement. Glue 3"–5" sprigs among the upper grapes. Loop
and glue the right ribbon tail downward among the hydrangea
and lower grapes, as shown in the large photo at right.

74" ivy, twig and rope garland
3 yards of 2" wide navy sheer ribbon with gold edges
10–12 strands of naturally colored raffia, each
    36"–45" long
3 stems of blue latex morning glories, each with a 24"
    section of seven 2½" long blossoms and many leaves
5 stems of rust silk azara, each with three 11"–17"
    sprigs of 4" long blossom clusters
3 oz. of naturally colored dried koolseed grass
30-gauge wire
glue gun and sticks or tacky craft glue

1 Find the garland center and mark with wire. Measure 6" on each side from the center and attach a wire loop hanger (see page 12). This will ensure that the garland hangs in a tight arch shape; if a wider arch is desired, attach the hangers farther from the center. Cut two morning glory stems to 26". Wire one on each side of the garland with the top leaf extending to the garland end.

2 Cut the last morning glory stem into two 14" sprigs, one with three blossoms and one with four. Wire to extend in opposite directions from the garland center toward the ends.

3 Cut each azara stem to 20". Wire one near one end of the garland; wire a second to extend from the garland center toward the same end and overlap the first. Repeat on the other side. Cut the last into two 10" sprigs, one

with two blossoms and one with three. Wire one on each side of the top. Trim one end of the ribbon in an inverted V; measure 4" from the end and glue this spot to the garland end. Loop and glue the ribbon along the garland, tucking it down among the flowers. Trim the end as before, leaving 4" to extend beyond the end of the garland.

4 Use your fingernail to shred the raffia into very fine strands. Hold two together and glue over the ribbon, tucking it among the flowers and gluing in the same spots as the ribbon. As you reach the ends, overlap two more strands and knot together 4" from the ends; glue to the ribbon. Continue to tuck and glue, allowing the raffia ends to extend. Cut the koolseed into 5"–6" sprigs. Glue evenly spaced among the florals, similarly angled.

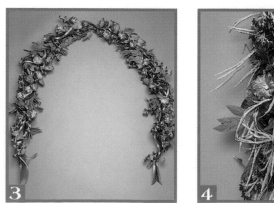

Magnolia Arch

24"x17" TWIGS™ arch
2 yards of 2½" wide green/gold lamé tapestry wire-edged ribbon
34" long silk magnolia spray with three 5" wide white blossoms and many 4"–6" green leaves
2 stems of green/dark blue latex formosa berries, each with three 3"–4" sprigs of ⅜"–⅝" berries and four 5"–6" leaves
2 stems of green latex grape ivy leaves, each with four 5"–7" sprigs of 2½"–3½" long leaves
2 oz. of light green dried avena or oats
30-gauge wire
glue gun and sticks or tacky craft glue

1 Cut away 15–20 twigs from the arch back and set aside for step 4. Shape the magnolia spray to follow the curve of the arch. Place it with the center blossom at the top of the arch and wire in several places to secure.

2 Cut the lowest 7" sprig off each grape leaf stem and set aside for step 4. Cut the remainder of each stem to 17" and wire one to curve down each side of the arch extending 1"–2" beyond the twig ends. Cut each berry stem to 15". Wire one to extend down the left side of the arch among the magnolia and grape leaves. Wire the other on the right end, extending along the outer edges of the magnolia spray. Shape the berries to

extend evenly among the leaves and blossoms.

3 Cut the ribbon into six 12" lengths. Use each length to make a ribbon loop (see page 21). Glue two loops behind the center magnolia, one angled to the upper right and one to the lower left. Glue two more evenly spaced on each side.

4 Glue one 7" leaf sprig from step 2 above the center magnolia, angled left, and one below the magnolia angled right. Cut the avena into 7"–10" sprigs; glue them and the twigs from step 1 evenly spaced along the arch, following the same angles as the other materials. Cut and glue 4"–6" sprigs around the center magnolia.

Shelf Garden

15"x14"x3" picket fence shelf
3½" long yellow mushroom bird
two ⅝" long speckled white plastic eggs
terra cotta pots: one 3½" and one 2¾" tall
1 green/pink silk wild epidendrum orchid plant with
    two 10"and one 7" tall flower branch, a 9" bud
    branch, ten 8"–11" wired leaves and exposed
    roots
1 white/yellow silk wild narcissus plant with two
    11"–12" branches of five 1" wide blossoms, six
    7"–11" wired leaves, a bulb and exposed roots
2 oz. of naturally colored dried rice grass
2 oz. of naturally colored dried poa grass or phalaris
2 oz. of green sheet moss
ivory acrylic paint, 1" wide paintbrush
spray wood sealer, gloss spray varnish
fine sandpaper
3"x3"x2" block of floral foam for silks
glue gun and sticks or tacky craft glue

1 Attach a sawtooth hanger to the shelf back. Sand the shelf and wipe clean. Spray with wood sealer; let dry. Paint it ivory and let dry. Sand again lightly, then varnish. Cut the foam to fit the large pot and insert securely. Use wire cutters to carefully chip away the rim of the small pot and make a 1" wide notch in the rim; save the chips. Glue moss into each pot.

2 Glue the large pot upright in front of the right edge of the leftmost picket. Glue the small pot on its side beside the large one, angled right, with the notch at the lower left. Glue the chips in front of the small pot opening. Glue the bird and additional moss as shown.

3 Trim the stems of the narcissus and orchid plants to 2"; shape the branches and leaves naturally. Glue the narcissus into the left back of the large pot. Angle it back toward the pickets, then curve the flowers to the right. Glue the orchid into the right back of the pot, curving to the right. Be sure the roots and bulbs remain exposed and aren't hidden by moss.

4 Cut ½ oz. each of rice and poa grass into 9"–14" sprigs. Glue into the foam around the orchid and narcissus, following the angles established by the flower branches. Cut and insert 5"–7" grass sprigs near the front of the upright pot and around both pots; glue 3"–4" sprigs around the pots to extend forward and along the shelf. Glue 2" rice grass sprigs and the eggs into the small pot.

24" long TWIGS™ broom
2½ yards of 3" wide dark plum wire-edged taffeta ribbon
3 stems of purple silk peonies, each with a 4" and a 2½"
    wide blossom and many leaves
2 stems of white silk daisies, each with three 9"–12"
    sprigs of many ¾" wide blossoms and leaves
2 stems of dark green silk ferns, each with nine 3½"–4"
    long leaves
2 oz. of naturally colored dried wheat
2 oz. of green preserved plumosus fern
30-gauge wire, glue gun and sticks or tacky craft glue

Broom Full of Spring Flowers

1 Cut one lower leaf from each silk fern stem; set aside for step 4. Trim the remaining stems to 15" and wire as shown, with one extending to the end of the twigs and the other toward the handle. Trim excess stem above the handle.

2 Cut a 2½" peony blossom from one stem and set aside for step 4. Cut the peony stems to 18", 14" and 12". Wire the 18" stem over the fern extending to the twig ends. Wire the 12" peony stem on the right and the 14" on the left.

3 Cut a 3-blossom daisy sprig from the lower area of one stem and set aside for step 4. Cut the stem to 16" and wire to the right side. Cut the other daisy stem to 18" and wire to the left side. Bend the sprigs to extend evenly among the peony and fern sprigs. Trim away any excess flower stems at the bottom of the handle.

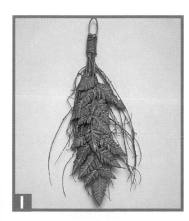

4 Use the ribbon to make a puffy bow (see page 20) with a center loop, six 4" loops and 10"–12" tails. Glue angled right over the stems at the handle. Glue one fern leaf from step 1 below the bow, angled down, and the other sprigs from steps 1–3 above the bow, angled upward. Glue 3"–6" wheat sprigs evenly spaced among the lower flowers, positioning them near materials of similar lengths. Glue 2" wheat sprigs above and around the bow. Glue 3"–6" plumosus sprigs among the flowers and bow loops.

32"x13" TWIGS™ wall plaque
6 stems of dark purple silk parrot tulips, each with a 4" tall
    blossom and 2 leaves
2 stems of black mini berries, each with fifteen 8"–11" sprigs
    of many ¼" wide berries
4½ yards of 3" wide dark purple shimmering taffeta wire-edged ribbon
4 oz. of dusty green preserved eucalyptus
5 oz. of naturally colored dried poppies
2 oz. of naturally colored dried silver king
30-gauge wire, glue gun and sticks or tacky craft glue

1 Cut each berry stem to 23" long. Position one over the bar of the plaque extending toward the left end. Place the second extending toward the right end. The sprigs should extend 4"–5" beyond the end of the bar. Wire each stem in two places to secure. Cut two tulips to 15" and four to 9". Wire the 15" tulips end to end over the berry stems with the stems overlapping 2" in the center. Wire two 9" tulips over each 15" stem. Curve all to angle slightly downward.

2 Use the ribbon to make a puffy bow (see page 20) with a center loop, six 4½" loops and 20" tails. Glue the bow to the plaque center over the flower stems. Cut the eucalyptus into 7"–11" sprigs and glue evenly spaced among the tulips and berries, following similar angles. Glue 5"–6" eucalyptus sprigs around the bow. Pull berry sprigs forward among the flowers and eucalyptus, curving them to extend naturally among the other materials.

3 Cut the poppies to 5"–9"; glue them evenly spaced among the tulips, eucalyptus and bow loops, following the same angles. Cut the silver king into 6"–10" sprigs and glue as for the poppies, as shown above. Attach a wire loop hanger to the upper back (see page 12).

Windowbox Filled with Wisteria

24"x12" TWIGS™ window with a 3" deep box
2 stems of lavender silk wisteria, each with three
*   8"–13" blossom heads and many leaves*
3 stems of silk wild blackberries, each with three
*   11"–14" sprigs of ⅝" long berries and many leaves*
1 green latex fern plant with nine 8"–9" fronds and 2
*   brown curled center sprigs*
1 oz. of naturally colored dried rice grass
1 oz. of green sheet moss
U-shaped floral pins, 30-gauge wire
3"x3"x3" block of floral foam for silks
glue gun and sticks or tacky craft glue

1 Cut the foam to fit into the left end of the box. Cover it with moss, securing with U-pins. Insert the foam into the box; if it isn't securely wedged in place, wire it. Shape one wisteria stem to follow the curve of the window and wire it to extend up the left side, over the top. The longest blossom head should curve halfway down the right side.

2 Shape a berry stem to follow the curve of the window top and wire it in front of the wisteria with the top berry positioned just past the window center. Cut the other wisteria stem to 25". Insert it into the left end of the foam to extend up the left side in front of the first stem, letting the leaves and flowers hang naturally.

3 Trim a berry stem to 18" and insert in front of the second wisteria; shape the sprigs to extend naturally among the wisteria. Trim the fern stem to 2". Insert it right of the wisteria, but still near the left end of the foam. Shape the fronds to extend naturally over the box edges.

4 Cut the remaining berry stem into one 10" and two 5" sprigs. Insert the 10" sprig into the foam right of the fern and shape it to extend over the front of the box, angled right. Insert a 5" sprig left of the fern and one right of the fern. Cut the rice grass into 8"–20" sprigs; insert around the fern near materials of similar lengths and at similar angles. Attach a wire hanger to the upper back (see page 12).

Baskets Abloom

Made from rattan, wicker, wood, palm fiber, wire and numerous other materials, baskets provide a warm feeling to any home. Even though a country decorating scheme comes immediately to mind when we think of baskets, they fit into other decorating styles just as well. Romantic or Victorian decorating features baskets containing lots of dried flowers along with silk roses, lilacs and pansies or other old-fashioned blooms. When we see a basket made from birch logs or bark, we think of the frontier or lodge look, while a green wire basket reminds us of the garden.

Many baskets are designed to hang on walls, with flat backs and some sort of hanger—maybe just a hole in the weave or a loop made of the basket material. A vertical design can be created by wiring these one above the other, then filling them with flowers which spill over the rims and down into the lower baskets. Using baskets of graduated sizes adds interest to the design.

A higher, more dynamic centerpiece can be achieved by stacking sitting baskets. Make sure they coordinate well or that's the only part of the design which will be noticed! Offset the baskets from each other and let the floral materials "waterfall" from one to the next.

If only one end of an oblong or oval basket is decorated, the other end remains usable for mail or towels or potpourri—or moss, a bird's nest and a bird can be tucked down into the empty area. Balls made of natural materials such as vines, or covered with moss, raffia, leaves, potpourri or spices can be stacked in the empty end to add intrigue, forcing the viewer to look through the design to discover all the components.

Attaching a small nosegay of silk and dried flowers to the handle turns an ordinary basket into something special. The cluster can be attached near the rim on one side, or to the top of the handle extending down each side. Add a bow and you have a great gift or decorating accent!

If you plan to fill a basket with an arrangement, keep in mind that the larger the basket is, the more materials it will take to fill it. Also, the height of the handle determines how long the stems should be to balance the design. Generally they should extend above the handle for a rich, abundant look. Be sure to consider the basket color when choosing flowers; they should coordinate to make sure the design is seen as a whole and not as separate elements.

Baskets are plentiful and can be found in a variety of sizes, shapes, colors, finishes, and materials. They add texture to a floral design and warmth to a room. The immense number of styles available make it easy for you to create a unique and gorgeous design!

A Well-Used Basket

10"x8"x4" oval rattan basket
3" long white mushroom bird
two 3" tall terra cotta clay pots
2 stems of yellow/peach silk snapdragons, each
    with a 17" section of blossoms and leaves
2 stems of red silk wild blackberries, each with
    3 sprigs of ¾" wide berries and many wired
    leaves
1 pink silk heather vine with a 20" section of
    1½" wide clusters of pellet-like blossoms
2 oz. of bromus secalinus grass
2 oz. of birch branches
two 3"–4" wide dried sponge mushrooms
4 oz. of green sheet moss
U-shaped floral pins
glossy walnut spray stain
3"x4"x6" block of floral foam for silks
glue gun and sticks or tacky craft glue

1 Use wire cutters to make a hole in the basket near the left front. Make another hole at the center back. Partially destroy the handles as well. Cut the foam to fit the left end of the basket and glue in place. Glue the mushrooms on the right front, small over large. Glue moss tufts randomly to the outside of the basket, between and on the mushrooms. Cover the foam sides with moss, securing with U-pins. Fill the basket with moss.

2 Use wire cutters to carefully chip the pot rims. Lightly spray the pots with stain, letting it spatter. Glue a moss tuft in each, then position them in the basket as shown. Cut one snapdragon to 18" and insert into the foam center, curving right. Cut the other stem to 14"; insert it right of the 18" stem, curving right.

3 Lightly spray the berries with stain to darken them. Cut one to 15" long; insert it left of the flowers, then shape the sprigs to extend among the blossoms. Cut the other into an 8" and a 10" sprig. Insert the 8" sprig right of the snapdragons extending upward. Insert the 10" sprig into the right side to extend horizontally through the basket.

4 Cut the top 12" off the heather stem; insert it into the side front to extend through the front hole, right and over the mushrooms. Cut the rest of the stem to 10"; insert it into the back to extend right along the rim. Cut the grass and birch branches to 7"–19". Insert as shown near materials of similar lengths. Cover any exposed foam with moss. Glue the bird to the right basket rim.

Doily & Roses Basket

10"x4" round rattan basket with a 7" tall handle
12" round ecru crocheted doily
2 yards of 2⅝" wide dark mauve/gold/green ribbon
6 stems of dark mauve silk roses, each with a 1½" tall blossom and 3 leaves
¼ oz. of naturally colored dried brisa media grass
8" of 24-gauge wire
glue gun and sticks or tacky craft glue

1 Fold down 5½" of the doily. Glue one end of the fold to the left basket rim 2" behind the handle. Bring the fold around the handle and glue to the basket front, wrapping it over the rim to the inside.

2 Use the ribbon to make an oblong bow (see page 20) with a center loop, six 2½"–4" loops, an 8" and a 13" tail. Angle the bow to wrap around the inside left handle base with the long tail extending to the back; glue. Loop and glue the short tail down the basket side.

3 Cut a rose to 2" and glue behind the bow extending downward beside the handle base. Cut the remaining roses as follows: one 5", one 4", two 3" and one 2". Glue the 5" rose curving over the front rim, extending from under the bow. Glue the 4" rose over it, angled slightly downward, and the two 3" roses over the 4" rose. Glue the 2" rose at the bow, covering all the stem ends.

4 Cut 3"–6" brisa media sprigs. Glue the longer sprigs near the longer roses and shorter sprigs around the 2" roses. Glue more 3"–4" sprigs among the bow loops and behind the bow.

Daisies & Marshberries

13"x6" bleached white wicker basket with a 7" tall handle

1 yard of 1½" wide navy satin wire-edged ribbon

1 stem of white silk daisies with fourteen 1"–1½" wide blossoms and 7 leaves

1 stem of dark blue artificial marshberries with eighteen 1½" wide clusters of pellet-like berries

2 oz. of green preserved ming fern

2 oz. of naturally colored preserved mini poppies

30-gauge wire

glue gun and sticks or tacky craft glue

1 Cut the fern into 3"–4" sprigs. Glue them along the basket rim, beginning at the right side of the handle and extending to the center front. Glue more extending back from the handle to the center back.

2 Wrap wire around the ribbon every 4". Glue the first wired spot 4" from one end of the glued fern. Tuck the ribbon among the fern sprigs and glue the wired areas to the rim, spacing them evenly.

3 Cut the daisies with 1" stems. Glue them evenly spaced among the fern sprigs, alternating them to angle inside and outside of the basket. Cut the remaining leaves off the main stem and glue them evenly spaced among the fern sprigs, positioning each to extend from under a daisy.

4 Cut the berry clusters with 1" stems. Glue them tucked down evenly among the fern and daisy sprigs. Cut the poppies into 2"–3" sprigs. Glue them evenly spaced among all the materials, alternating the angles as for the daisies.

Sunflowers & Acorns Basket

10"x7" palm fiber basket with 2
   short handles
4½ yards of ⅝" wide jute/string
   wired braid
two 20" long golden pheasant
   feathers
four 48" long naturally colored raffia strands
1 cream silk sunflower stem with a
   4" wide blossom of wired petals
   and 3 wired leaves
1 wired stem of flocked nuts with a
   14" section of twelve ¾" wide
   nuts and many 2½" long green
   and brown silk wired leaves
½ oz. of green sheet moss
30-gauge wire
glue gun and sticks or tacky craft
   glue

1 Cut the nut stem to 15". Insert it from top to bottom through one handle until the lowest sprig is below the handle. Wire in two places to secure, then curve the stem to follow the basket front. Cut an 11" long upper portion from one feather and 13" from the other. Insert both through the handle and glue over the nut stem.

2 Cut the feather bottoms to 5" and 6½"; glue them over the upper ends, extending downward as shown. Cut the sunflower with a 2" stem. Glue it to extend out the bottom of the handle with the stem angled toward the basket back. Cut off the leaves; glue one to cover the stem end, one below the flower and one to the right of the flower over the nut stem.

3 Hold the raffia over the braid and handle as one. Make a puffy bow (see page 20) with a center loop, eight 3½" loops and 18" tails. Use your fingernail to shred the raffia loops and tails. Knot each set of raffia tails together near the ends.

4 Glue the bow behind the sunflower, then loop one tail with its raffia toward the back; glue to hold. Loop and glue the other tail along the lower front. Glue moss tufts over stem ends and wires to cover them.

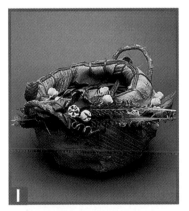

A Basket with a Rustic Touch

16"x10" round lacquered rattan basket with a 10" tall handle

2⅓ yards of 2½" wide rust/dark green tapestry wire-edged ribbon

3 stems of rust silk sunflowers, each with a 3" wide blossom and 5 leaves

2 stems of yellow silk sunflowers, each with a 3" wide blossom and 5 leaves

2 stems of latex acorns, each with five 1" green/brown nuts and 6 leaves

2 stems of green silk sprengeri, each with a 15" section of 4"–5" sprigs

1 stem of gold artificial heather with 3 branches of nine 3" long sprigs with many pellet-like blossoms

30-gauge wire

glue gun and sticks or tacky craft glue

1 Cut the rust sunflowers to 15", 9" and 7". Cut the yellow sunflowers to 12" and 5". Save the leaves. Beginning 6" above the basket rim, wire the 15", 12" and 7" sunflowers to extend up the right side of the handle over the center top as shown. Wire the 9" sunflower to extend down to the right rim with the 5" stem just above it.

2 Cut one sprengeri stem to 18" and wire to extend 1"–2" beyond the 15" sunflower. Cut the upper 11" off the other stem and wire to extend downward below the lowest sunflower. Set the rest aside for step 4. Cut the heather into a 9", a 10" and a 12" sprig. Wire the 12" sprig to extend between the 12" and 15" sunflowers. Wire the 10" sprig to extend behind the 7" sunflower. Wire the 9" sprig to extend downward between the two lowest flowers.

3 Cut one nut stem to 15" and wire to extend 2" beyond the 15" sunflower. Cut the upper 7" off the other stem and wire upward just behind the 7" flower. Cut the rest of that stem to 11" and wire to extend downward below the lowest flower.

4 Use the ribbon to make a flat bow (see page 19) with a center loop, two 3¼" and two 4" loops, an 18" and a 27" tail. Wire and glue it at an angle over the stems 8" above the rim. Tuck and glue the long tail over the handle and the short one down the basket side. Glue sprengeri sprigs and any leftover leaves around the bow to hide wires and fill empty spaces.

Sunflower Wall Basket

- 11"x9"x4" rattan wall basket
- 3 stems of yellow silk ox-eye sunflowers, each with six 2"–2½" wide blossoms and many leaves
- 1 yellow silk sunflower stem with a 4" wide blossom of wired petals and 3 leaves
- 1 stem of burgundy/rust/green latex crabapples with an 18" and two 8" sprigs of ½"–¾" wide apples and wired leaves
- 3 stems of burgundy/orange/rust latex fall leaves, each with five 2½"–3" wide leaves and 2 berry clusters
- three 6"–9" golden pheasant feathers
- one 3" wide dried pomegranate on a pick
- two 4"–5" naturally colored dried chili peppers
- 4 oz. of naturally colored dried bearded wheat or barley
- three 2½" wired wood picks
- 1 oz. of green sheet moss
- U-shaped floral pins
- 6"x4"x3" block of floral foam for silks
- glue gun and sticks or tacky craft glue

1 Cut and glue the foam to fit the left side of the basket. Cover the sides with moss, securing with U-pins. Cut one ox-eye sunflower stem to 17", one to 15", and one into two 10" sprigs, each with three blossoms. Curve the 17" stem to the right and insert into the foam back, extending upward. Curve the 15" stem to the right; insert it into the front to extend downward and curve back toward the left side. This forms the base for an S or "Hogarth" curve.

2 Insert one 10" sprig in front of the 17" stem; insert the last sprig to extend forward over the 15" stem. Cut a leaf stem to 17", curve it and insert it left of the 17" sunflower stem following the same lines. Cut a 16" leaf stem; curve and insert it right of the lower sunflowers. Cut the upper 8" off the last leaf stem and insert in front of the upright 10" sunflower sprig. Cut the rest of that stem to 7" and insert left of the lower sunflowers.

3 Cut the upper 16" off the crabapple stem and insert in front of the upper 17" sunflower stem. Cut the rest to 14" and insert to extend among the lower sunflowers. Cut the yellow sunflower stem to 6". Insert it in front of the upright materials, extending forward and slightly right. Insert the remaining leaves around the stem.

4 Attach a wood pick to one feather; insert behind the large sunflower, curving right. Insert a feather to the left and one to extend forward among the lower materials (see arrows). Attach a wood pick to each pepper (see page 14). Insert them and the pomegranate in a cluster at the left front corner as shown. Cut the wheat into 6"–16" stems. Insert evenly spaced among materials of similar lengths. Glue moss to cover any exposed foam.

Climbing Roses & Twigs

27" tall TWIGS™ wall basket (about 17" wide)
1¼ yards of 1¼" wide pale green sheer wire-edged
* ribbon*
2 stems of yellow silk climbing roses, each with four
* 1"–2" wide blossoms and many wired leaves*
1 stem of purple silk/latex pokeberries with a 15" and
* 19" branch of two or three 5" sprigs of ¼"–⅜"*
* wide berries and many wired leaves*
1 stem of white silk daisies with 4 sprigs of 1"–1¼"
* wide blossoms and 4" long leaves*
1 oz. of light green dried wild oats
3–4 oz. of green sheet moss
one 2½" wired wood pick
glue gun and sticks or tacky craft glue

1 Stuff the basket tightly with moss, filling it to the rim. Glue small tufts randomly over the outside of the basket and to the lower areas of a few upper twigs. Cut one rose stem to 19". Insert it into the basket slightly right of center. Shape the sprigs naturally. Cut the upper two roses and bud off the second stem and to 8". Cut the rest of the stem into an 11" sprig. Insert the 11" sprig in front of the 19" stem, extending upward. Insert the 8" sprig into the front of the basket between twigs, curving forward and down.

2 Cut the pokeberry into an 11" long 2-sprig and a 20" long 3-sprig branch. Insert the 20" branch left of the upright roses and the 11" branch right of them. Cut an 8" and a 9" sprig off the daisy stem. Cut the rest of the stem to 14". Insert it among the roses on the left side. Insert the 9" sprig at the right of the roses. Insert the 8" sprig in front of the roses, angled forward.

3 Measure 14" from one end of the ribbon and wire this point to the wood pick. Trim each ribbon end in a V, then insert the pick into the moss right of the roses. Loop and drape the long tail upward among the roses and berries; loop the short tail among the lower roses.

4 Cut 5"–21" wild oat sprigs; insert them evenly spaced among materials of similar lengths with the shortest sprigs extending forward over the lower roses, but not down among them. Attach a wire loop hanger to the basket back (see page 12).

Basket of Roses

8"x6"x4" oval vine basket with a 5" tall handle

1 yard of 2⅝" wide pink/sage green/cream tapestry wire-edged ribbon

9 stems of pink silk roses, each with a 3½" wide blossom and 3 sprigs of 5 wired leaves

3 stems of lavender silk clover, each with 3 sprigs of five 1" blossoms and 6 leaves

3 oz. of dark green preserved leatherleaf fern

2 oz. of naturally colored dried brisa maxima grass

2 oz. of brown American Moss™ excelsior

U-shaped floral pins

8" of 24 gauge wire

two 3"x4"x8" blocks of floral foam for silks

glue gun and sticks or tacky craft glue

(side view) 9" 10" 9" 8" 8"

(top view) 9" 8" 8" 10" 9" 9" 8" 8" 9"

1 Trim the foam blocks to fit in the basket. U-pin moss around the outer sides if the foam can be seen through the basket vines. Insert the covered foam into the basket. Cut one rose to 10" and insert upright into the center. Cut four roses to 8"; insert evenly spaced around the basket to extend horizontally from the foam sides. Cut four stems to 9". Insert them evenly spaced between the 10" and 8" roses angling outward 45°. Cut the remaining leaves with 1"–2" stems; insert evenly spaced around the rim and near the 9" roses.

2 Cut a 10" clover sprig off each of two stems. Insert one on each side of the 10" rose, slightly angled toward the basket ends. Cut four 8" and three 9" sprigs. Insert the 8" sprigs among the 8" rose stems and the 9" clover sprigs among the 9" rose stems at similar angles.

3 Cut 9"–11" fern sprigs. Insert evenly near materials of similar lengths. Repeat with 9"–12" lengths of brisa maxima. U-pin moss to cover any exposed foam.

4 Use the ribbon to make a puffy bow (see page 20) with a center loop, two 3" loops and 7" tails. Wire and glue the bow to one side of the handle 4" above the basket rim.

Garden Wall Basket

12"x14" TWIGS™ flat wall basket
5 strands of naturally colored raffia, 50"–60" long
3 stems of dark mauve silk ranunculus, each with a 3" and a 2" wide blossom and many wired flocked leaves
1 stem of green latex ivy with three 18" sections of 1¼"–2½" wide wired leaves and brown stems
1 stem of silk wild blackberries with three 11"–14" sprigs of ⅝" long berries and many wired leaves
2 oz. of green preserved plumosus
30-gauge wire
glue gun and sticks or tacky craft glue

1 Cut the ivy into three 18" sprigs. Wire one to extend from the left basket rim up the handle past the center top. Wire the second to extend diagonally across the basket front from left to lower right. Cut the last sprig into an 11" and a 7" sprig. Wire the 11" sprig to extend from the left across the rim; wire the 7" sprig from the left rim down the left side of the basket.

2 Cut the berry stem into a 13", a 12" and a 9" sprig. Wire the 13" sprig up the left handle. Wire the 12" berry sprig diagonally across the basket front above the 18" ivy sprig and the 9" berry sprig diagonally below it.

3 Cut a ranunculus to 13" and wire to extend up the handle over the berries and ivy. Cut the 3" blossom sprig from the second ranunculus stem to 5" long and the 2" one to 8" long. Glue or wire the 8" sprig diagonally across the basket over the 18" ivy. Glue the 5" sprig to extend from the left handle above the 8" sprig. Cut the 3" blossom of the last stem to 5" long and the 2" blossom to 6" long. Glue the 6" sprig to extend up the left handle. Glue the 5" sprig angled down the handle, positioning the blossom just below the basket rim. Cut the remaining leaves off the ranunuculus stems and glue at the left side of the basket to cover any wires.

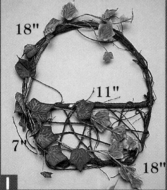

4 Cut the plumosus into 6"–12" sprigs and glue evenly spaced among all the materials. Dampen a raffia strand and set aside. Hold the remaining strands together and make a raffia collar bow (see page 119) with 3" loops and 14"–17" tails. Secure with the damp strand, then shred all the loops and tails with your fingernail. As shown in the large photo, glue the bow over the stems at the left side of the basket handle. Weave the tails on the right among the materials diagonally across the basket.

A Basket of Spring Flowers

12"x6½"x4½" whitewashed basket with a 13"
   tall handle
2¼ yards of 2½" wide blue/light yellow/green
   printed ribbon
3 stems of blue silk and latex Dutch iris, each with
   a 5" wide blossom, a heavy stem and 3 leaves
1 green latex fern plant with fourteen 11"–14"
   fronds and two curled fiddleheads
2 white silk narcissus plants, each with two 3"
   wide clusters of five 1" wide blossoms, 6 leaves
   and a bulb with roots
2 white silk wild hyacinth plants, each with a stem
   of white blossoms in a 5" long cluster, 3 leaves
   and a bulb with roots
7 oz. of green preserved wild boxwood
2 oz. of green American Moss™ excelsior
U-shaped floral pins
one 3" wired wood pick
two 4"x3"x8" blocks of floral foam for silks
8" of 24-gauge wire
glue gun and sticks or tacky craft glue

1 Cut the floral foam to fit in the basket extending 1" above the rim; glue in place. Cut an iris to 19", one to 15" and one to 13". Insert the 19" iris close to the right end of the basket, curving slightly left. Insert the 15" left of the first, curving forward and left. Insert the 13" stem directly behind the 15" stem curving toward the left back.

2 Cover the foam with moss, securing with U-pins. Cut the stem of the fern to 3" and insert into the foam at the left end of the basket. Angle it over the left side and curve the fronds to extend over the front, back and left end of the basket.

3 Cut the bulb stem wires of the hyacinths to 3". Insert both between the fern and the iris, extending forward and curving left. Turn the basket around to view the back. Cut the bulb stem wires of the narcissus to 3" and insert them right of the iris, again curving toward the fern and over the basket edge. Turn the basket to face you again.

4 Use the ribbon to make a puffy bow (see page 20) with a center loop, six 3¾" loops and 9" tails. Attach the bow to a wood pick, then insert at the right front corner beside the iris. Pull one tail to the back and let the other drape down the front. Cut the boxwood into 18"–5" sprigs. Insert them evenly spaced near materials of similar lengths.

back view

Autumn Harvest Centerpiece

16"x9"x6½" TWIGS™ basket with a 4" handle on each end
1⅔ yards of 2⅞" wide gold/brown printed ribbon with gold lamé lining and gold wired edges
1 green/rust silk ivy plant with seven 9"–36" branches of 1"–2¾" wide leaves
1 stem of purple latex grapes with a 10" section of ⅝"–⅞" grapes and 5 leaves
1 stem of latex peaches with a 3" and a 2" peach, a 2" peach quarter and many wired leaves
1 latex fruit stem with a 4" pear, two 2" red pomegranates, 2 pine cones and grape leaves
1 yellow/green 4" pear-shaped latex gourd with 3 leaves
two 5" wide artificial pumpkins: 1 orange, 1green
3 oz. of red preserved heather
3 oz. of naturally colored dried avena (or oats)
3 oz. of naturally colored dried large chili peppers
2 oz. of green sheet moss
U-shaped floral pins, 3" wired wood picks
six 3"x4"x8" blocks of floral foam for silks
glue gun and sticks or tacky craft glue

1 Cut the foam to fit the basket, extending 1" above the rim. Cover the outer edges with moss, securing with U-pins. Insert the ivy into the right back corner. Pin two longer branches to curve over the foam and down the front near the left end. Shape a long branch to extend along the back and side of the rim and side. Shape the shorter branches to extend upward naturally, curving over the foam and the right end.

2 Insert the grape stem into the left front corner to extend down the side. Cut the peach and pear branches to 20". Insert the pear branch in front of the ivy stem; curve it to extend across the foam to the back left corner. Insert the peach branch in front of the pear and shape it to extend across the foam to the left front.

3 If the pumpkins do not have picks, make a hole with a knife point in the bottom and glue in a wood pick. Insert the green pumpkin over the peach and pear stems and the orange one angled over the basket front right rim. Insert the gourd into the foam at the right end, extending under the handle and over the rim.

4 Loop and tuck the ribbon left to right through the design, allowing one end to trail on the table at each end. Cut a 14" heather sprig and hold together with two 13" avena sprigs; wire to a wood pick. Insert this cluster among the materials, angled left. Repeat, making 8"–14" clusters; insert evenly among all the materials at similar angles. Glue chili peppers to fill empty spaces. Glue moss to cover any exposed foam.

Hydrangeas in a Log Basket

12"x7"x7" flat-backed log wall basket with a 7" tall handle
2⅓ yards of 1½" wide purple/blue variegated wire-edged ribbon
three 60" naturally colored raffia strands
2 stems of purple silk campanula, each with a 13" section of 2" long bell-like blossoms and buds
2 stems of blue/purple silk hydrangeas, each with a 6" wide head of 1" wide blossoms and 9 leaves
2 stems of purple silk wildflowers, each with three 9" sprigs of ¾" wide blossoms
2 stems of dark green latex rose leaves, each with 3 sprigs of six 2"–2½" long leaves
4 oz. of green preserved buck foliage
2 oz. of naturally colored dried ting ting
2 oz. of brown American Moss® excelsior
two 4"x3"x8" blocks of floral foam for silks
U-shaped floral pins
one 3" wired wood pick
glue gun and sticks or tacky craft glue

1 Cut the foam to fit the basket, extending ½" above the front rim. Glue in place, then tuck moss between the slats to cover exposed foam. Pin more moss around the upper front edges. Cut a campanula stem to 20" and insert it upright into the center back foam. Cut the second stem to 17"; insert it in front and right of the first stem.

2 Cut one hydrangea to 14" and insert 2" left of the first campanula stem. Cut the second hydrangea to 10". Insert in front and right of the 14" stem. Cut the buck foliage to 13"–17" long. Insert into the foam in a cluster right of the campanula.

3 Cut one wildflower stem to 14" and insert in front of the campanula and buck foliage. Cut the other into three 9½" sprigs; insert around the front of the first, angled forward. Cut one rose leaf stem to 13". Insert it at the left back corner of the foam, then bend it to curve forward around the top of the basket rim. Cut the other into a 7" and two 6" sprigs. Insert between the hydrangea and the 13" rose leaf stem.

4 Cover any exposed foam with moss, securing with U-pins. Hold a raffia strand over the ribbon to make a puffy bow (see page 20) with a center loop, eight 3" loops, a 10" and a 15" tail. Shred the raffia with your fingernail, attach the bow to a wood pick, then insert it at the right front corner with the tails extending over the side. Cut the ting ting into 10"–23" lengths and insert into the foam evenly spaced near materials of similar lengths as shown in the large photo.

Florals Sitting Pretty

The beginning point of designing a floral piece which sits, such as a centerpiece, topiary or floor accent, is to select a base. To turn an ordinary object into a base for floral designing, attach a block of floral foam—its size depends on how large the design will be. Items such as bird cages and houses, twig bundles, and papier-mâché boxes all can be effective bases, adding interest, texture or a theme to a pretty collection of silk and dried flowers.

Sometimes a centerpiece (designed to be viewed from all sides) isn't needed; maybe the design will be sitting on a table against a wall. In such a case the back should be flat, allowing the piece to nestle against the wall and take up less room. Make sure it is finished, though, with all the mechanics covered or hidden; don't leave exposed foam, stem ends and wires that may be seen from the sides.

The bases chosen for this book include everything from baskets for the country look, birch branches for a woodsy effect, and a birdhouse in the garden style, to decorated papier-mâché boxes for a rich and upscale appearance. If it sits, it can be decorated with florals and made into a table decoration or centerpiece! And if the base, be it a basket or a plastic vase, isn't the desired color or texture, there are products available to change that. Use granite paint for texture, or swirls of paint to add coordinating colors. Glue twigs, raffia or rope around a plastic vase to change the look from modern to country or rustic.

Working in harmony with the shape and style of the base allows the entire design to blend, creating a feeling of completeness and continuity. Make sure the base looks country if the floral design uses country-type flowers such as sunflowers, wildflowers, peonies, mums, etc. By the same token, if you are working toward an elegant look, use magnolias or large roses to provide it—and, of course, use an elegant base such as a footed bowl or a metal basket.

The joke is that if something holds still long enough we'll put a floral decoration on it. That's not far from the truth. Baskets, boxes, branches, birdhouses and cages, candle bases, watering cans—nothing is safe from being decorated with florals!

Nested Ball & Birds

TWIGS™ vine balls: one 12", one 6"
two 4" long blue/white mushroom birds
4 stems of dark purple/green silk mulberries, each
    with a 10" section of ten 1" long berries and
    many wired leaves
2 stems of pink silk heather vine, each with an
    18" section of many 1½" wide clusters of pel-
    let-like blossoms and many leaves
1 oz. of dark green preserved maidenhair fern
    (about 10 stems)
1 oz. of gray American Moss® excelsior
U-shaped floral pins
4"x3"x3" block of floral foam for silks
30-gauge wire
glue gun and sticks or tacky craft glue

1 Use wire cutters to make a hole in the front of the large ball big enough for the 6" ball to fit through. Slip the 6" ball inside and wire it to the base, positioning it closer to the left side. Cut the floral foam to fit between the right sides of the balls. Cover the foam with moss and secure with U-pins, then wedge it in place. Make a nest from a handful of moss and glue it into the bottom of the small ball.

2 Cut one berry stem to 16". Insert it through the large ball top and into the foam; curve it to follow the ball shape over the center top, angled left. Wire to secure. Cut a 13" berry stem. Insert it into the foam side and curve it to climb the right side of the large ball among the first berry sprigs; wire. Cut a 14" berry stem. Insert it into the front of the foam to extend out the opening and curve left along the lower front of the ball.

3 Cut the last stem into a 7" and a 6" sprig. Insert the 7" sprig into the foam top and curve it to extend over the top of the small ball. Insert the 6" sprig through the right side of the large ball to extend upward in front of the previous stems. Cut a 19" heather stem. Insert it into the lower front of the foam through the large ball. Curve it to extend forward and along the lower front of the small ball; wire to secure. Cut the last heather stem to 18". Insert and curve it as for the 16" berry stem, weaving it around the berry stem.

4 Glue a bird into the nest in the small ball. Glue the other bird among the berries and heather on the upper right side of the large ball. Cut 3"–5" fern sprigs and glue them evenly spaced among all the materials. Cut three 2"–3" sprigs and glue them around the nesting bird. Glue small moss tufts to cover exposed foam or wires.

9"x8 ½"x7" bark bird-
  house
two 6" long peach/tan
  feathered birds
2 stems of peach fabric
  dogwood, each with five
  2 ½" wide blossoms and
  8 wired leaves
1 stem of green latex grape
  leaves with seven 5"–8"
  sprigs of 1 ½"–2" wide
  wired leaves
1 stem of silk blackberries
  with three 9"–12"
  sprigs of ⅝" berries and
  many leaves
1 oz. of dark green pre-
  served leather fern
3 oz. of naturally colored
  dried centaurea
½ oz. of green sheet moss
3"x2"x1" block of floral
  foam for silks
glue gun and sticks or
  tacky craft glue

Dogwood & Berries on a Birdhouse

1 Trim the corners off the top of the foam and glue it to the right roof back next to the peak. Cut one dogwood stem to 16". Insert it into the foam front extending to the front right roof corner. Shape it to curve down to the right front corner of the base, then to the left. Cut the second dogwood into a 12" and an 8" sprig. Insert the 12" sprig into the foam center top. Shape it to curve down the roof and right house side, then forward. Insert the 8" sprig to extend left and forward over the roof top.

2 Cut the berry stem into a 9", an 11" and a 12" sprig. Insert the 12" sprig between the long dogwood sprigs, curving it to fit. Insert the 11" sprig to extend in front of the 16" dogwood and the 9" berry sprig into the foam front to curve forward left of the 16" dogwood stem (see arrows).

3 Cut the two lowest sprigs off the grape stem, trimming one to 5" and one to 6". Insert them into the foam top, one extending left along the short dogwood sprig and one extending forward, angled down. Cut the remaining stem to 14" and insert it into the foam in front of the 12" berry sprig. Shape the dogwood flowers to extend naturally among the berries and grape leaves.

4 Cut the fern into 4"–11" sprigs. Insert shorter ones to extend among the short dogwood sprigs and grape leaves. Insert the rest near materials of similar lengths. Repeat with the centaurea, cutting them into 4"–14" sprigs. Glue three 2"–3" fern and three 2"–3" centaurea sprigs onto the left front corner of the house, then glue a bird over them. Glue the second bird to the foam at the roof peak. Glue moss to cover any exposed foam, then glue a small tuft on each side of the lower bird and one into the door hole of the house.

3 old hardback books, each about 6"x8"
2⅔ yards of 2½" wide rust/gold tie-dyed satin wire-edged ribbon with creases
2 stems of white silk daisies, each with 4 sprigs of three 1½" wide blossoms and wired leaves
1 stem of rust/green burgundy/ latex rose hips with 3 sprigs of 1½" long hips and many wired leaves
1 stem of green/burgundy silk grape leaves with fourteen 2"–4" long leaves, tendrils and a brown stem with moss
1 oz. of naturally colored dried mustard grass
dark walnut wood stain, clean cloth. spray wood sealer
8" of 24-gauge wire
glue gun and sticks or tacky craft glue

1 Spray the books with the sealer and let dry. To make them look older, use the cloth to wipe on walnut stain, then wipe it off; repeat to the desired darkness. When dry, spray again with sealer. Glue in a stack, offsetting them as shown. The spines will be the front.

2 Glue one end of the ribbon at the center top of the stack; wrap the ribbon crosswise around the books. Allow the ends to overlap 2" and trim excess. Use the rest of the ribbon to make a puffy bow (see page 20) with six 4" loops, a 9" and a 10" tail. Glue to the top center books over the ribbon; ripple the tails down the sides.

3 Cut a 5" and a 6" daisy sprig off one stem (save excess leaves and blossoms). Glue both to extend from the bow center toward the back left corner. Repeat, gluing two sprigs extending toward the front right corner. Glue the leftover blossoms and leaves among the stems. Cut individual 2"–3" daisies off two sprigs of the remaining stem. Glue them into the bow center, extending upward

and over the stem ends of the previous sprigs. Glue leaves among these daisies.

4 Cut the grape leaves into 2- or 3-leaf sprigs. Glue them evenly spaced among the daisies, extending at similar angles and tucking the larger leaves under the flowers. Cut the rose hips into one 3" and two 5" sprigs. Glue one 5" sprig among the daisies on each end and the other among the center flowers; shape the leaves and hips to curve among the flowers. As shown above, cut the mustard grass into 4"–7" sprigs. Glue evenly spaced among all the materials at similar angles.

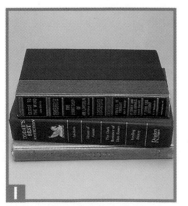

Garden in a Watering Can

8" tall metal watering can with a 5" tall handle
one 12" wide grapevine wreath
3 stems of mauve silk tulips, each with a 2¼"
    tall blossom and 2 leaves
2 stems of white silk carnations, each with five
    2" wide blossoms and 3 buds

1 stem of black/green latex poke-berries with a 21" section of ¼"–⅜" berries and many wired leaves
1 purple/green variegated purple passion bush with eighteen 8"–11" branches of 1½"–2" long leaves
1 oz. of green preserved tree fern
2 oz. of green mood moss
U-shaped floral pins
8"x4"x3" block of floral foam for silks
30-gauge wire, glue gun and sticks or tacky craft glue

1 Cut the foam to fit on end against the inner handle side of the can; glue in place. Cover the exposed sides with moss, securing with U-pins—leave the top bare for now. Cut the binding vines or wires off the wreath and pull it apart. Cut a section about 7 vines thick away from the rest; drape it over the can and wire it to the handle and spigot as shown. Set aside the rest of the vines.

2 Cut the tulips to 18", 16" and 13½" tall. Insert the 18" tulip into the foam center and shape to curve slightly left. Shape the other two to curve left, then insert the 16" stem to the right of the 18" stem, the 13½" to its left. Cut the pokeberry stem to 22". Insert behind the 18" tulip, shaping the sprigs to extend among the flowers.

3 Cut a carnation stem to 17". Insert it behind the 13½" tulip and shape the blossoms to extend forward among the tulips. Cut the other carnation to 13"; insert it in front of the 18" tulip. Shape the sprigs among the leaves and blossoms. Insert the passion bush at the front right corner. Shape two long branches to extend down the grape vines and one long branch to extend upward. Shape the others to spill over the can front and left edge.

4 Cut 6"–15" tree fern sprigs and insert around the tulips and carnations with longer sprigs in the center and shorter ones around the outside. Glue more moss to cover any exposed foam. Glue a 3" wide, 2" deep moss tuft to the outside lower right of the can. Glue ½"–1" tufts randomly to the grape vines nearest the floral materials and where the spout joins the can.

Adorned Treasure Box

9"x4" hexagon papier-mâché box
2¼" wide filigree brass heart
8" round cream crocheted doily
2⅓ yards of 1⅜" wide cream tapestry ribbon
½ oz. of naturally colored dried rice grass

3 stems of cream silk roses, each with a 2½" wide blossom, two 3-leaf sprigs and three 5-leaf sprigs
1 stem of pink silk rosebuds with five sprigs of three or six ¾" long buds
gold spray webbing
gold spray glitter

gloss spray varnish
acrylic paints: black, ivory
1" wide paintbrush
water container, paper towels
8" of 24-gauge wire
glue gun and sticks or tacky craft glue

1 Paint the box and lid ivory; let dry. Lightly spray both pieces with webbing; let dry. Spray the box and lid with varnish. Paint the heart black; let dry for one minute, then wipe the paint off, leaving some in the crevices. When it is completely dry, spray with varnish.

2 Glue the doily to the box lid. Use the ribbon to make a puffy bow (see page 20) with a center loop, ten 3" loops and 4" tails. Glue to the doily center. Glue the heart angled into the bow center as shown.

3 Cut the cream roses to 3" and glue among the bow loops as shown. Cut four 5-leaf sprigs to 5". Glue evenly spaced around the bow, extending from under the roses to just beyond the lid edge. Cut three 2½" long 3-leaf sprigs and glue evenly spaced among the bow loops around the heart.

4 Cut three 5-rosebud sprigs to 3" and glue around the bow between the cream roses. Cut two 3-bud sprigs to 2" and glue near the heart. As shown above, cut 4"–6" rice grass sprigs and glue evenly spaced among the previous materials. Position longer sprigs around the outside with shorter ones nearer the center. Spray the entire arrangement with glitter.

88 ~ Sitting Pretty

Spring Bulb Basket

9"x4" painted whitewashed round basket
   with an 8" tall handle
4" brown feathered fat robin
3" wide straw bird nest
three ⅝" long speckled plastic eggs
1 stem of red artificial mini berries with fifteen 9"–11" sprigs of ¼" berries
2 stems of blue silk Dutch iris, each with
   three 3" wide blossoms and 4 wired
   leaves
2 stems of silk wild narcissus, each with a
   bulb, 2 clusters of five 1½" wide blossoms, 6 wired leaves and brown fiber
   roots
1 stem of yellow/green silk wild epidendrum
   orchids with three 2½" wide blossoms, 1
   bud stem, 10 wired leaves and brown
   fiber roots
1 green silk ivy plant with twelve 7"–12"
   branches of 1"–2" wide leaves
1 oz. of green sheet moss
U-shaped floral pins
two 4"x3"x8" blocks of floral foam for silks
30-gauge wire
glue gun and sticks or tacky craft glue

1 Cut the foam to fit the basket, filling it level with the rim. Cover with moss and secure with U-pins. Cut two 12" ivy branches. Wire one to extend up the left handle over to the upper right. Insert the second branch into the foam at the left handle base and wire to cover the stem of the first branch.

2 Insert the rest of the ivy plant into the foam next to the left handle base. Wire one 12" branch along the front basket rim and another along the back rim. U-pin three 10" branches to "crawl" over the moss, spaced evenly apart. Shape short branches to extend over the rim, and the rest to "grow" naturally.

3 Cut one iris stem to 16" and one to 15". Insert the 16" stem into the foam behind the handle near the left side and the 15" stem in front of the handle. Cut the stems of the narcissus to 2". Insert them to the right of the iris, one angled to the right and one forward.

4 Cut the stem on the orchid to 2". Insert it into the foam behind the iris, angled over the back rim of the basket. Cut the berry stem into two 15" long sections. Insert one in front of the ivy at the left handle base and one behind the narcissus bulbs. Insert a U-pin through one side of the nest; insert the nest to the right of the narcissus bulbs, angled forward. Glue a moss tuft and the eggs into the nest and the bird onto the left side of the basket looking right.

back view

front view

Halloween Candy Basket

9"x7"x 3½" stained rectangular wicker basket with a 9" tall handle

2⅓ yards of 2¼" wide orange taffeta ribbon with gold wired edges

10–12 strands each of 40" long black and orange raffia

1 autumn-colored silk mixed flower bush with twelve 10"–13" branches of ¾"–3" wide blossoms and leaves

1 rust/green silk maple leaf bush with four 9" branches of many 1¾"–4" wide leaves and three ¾" wide naturally-colored pods

3 oz. of naturally-colored dried linum atraxa

2 oz. of brown American Moss® excelsior

wired wood picks: two 6", six 3"

U-shaped floral pins

3"x4"x6" block of floral foam for silks

glue gun and sticks or tacky craft glue

I Cut the foam to fit the left end of the basket with 1" extending above the rim. Glue in place, then cover with moss, securing with U-pins. Fill the empty end of the basket with moss. From the flower bush, cut the tallest branch to 13" and insert into the foam center. Cut six of the shortest flower bush branches to 9". Insert around the basket edge, extending almost parallel with the table. Leave the right side of the foam empty.

2 Cut the remaining flower branches to 12"; insert around the 13" branch and angled away from it. Hold a strand of black raffia over the ribbon and handle as one to make a puffy bow (see page 20) with a center loop, six 3" loops and 12" tails. Add more raffia as needed, then add two strands for extra tails. Shred the raffia with your thumbnail, then attach the bow to a 3" wood pick and insert into the empty space on the right side of the foam. Glue a ribbon tail on each side of the basket.

3 Cut 9" maple leaf branches off the stem. Insert one near the 13" flower branch and one to extend over the basket end. Insert one near each side of the handle. Hold one raffia strand of each color together. Form into 3"–4" loops (see page 119), then wire to a 6" wood pick. Repeat. Insert one set in front of and one behind the 13" flower branch.

4 Make five more raffia loop sets, attaching them to 3" picks. Insert evenly spaced among the 9" and 12" flower branches. Cut the linum into 6"–13" sprigs; insert evenly spaced near flower branches of similar lengths and angles. Fill the basket with candy for a pretty yet functional centerpiece.

Hurricane Centerpiece

6"x9½" white metal/glass hurricane base
1 yard of 1½" wide blue/purple variegated
   taffeta wire-edged ribbon
3 stems of blue/purple silk sweet peas, each with
   six 2" blossoms, 3 buds, many leaves and tendrils
1 green/white/mauve silk begonia bush with eighteen
   5"–15" branches of 1"–2" wide leaves
2 stems of silk blackberries, each with one 13" and
   two 9" sprigs of ¾" berries and many leaves
2 oz. of naturally colored dried silver king
4"x6"x2" block of floral foam for silks
1 oz. of Spanish moss, U-shaped floral pins
glue gun and sticks or tacky craft glue

1 Cut the floral foam into two pieces, then trim to fit around the hurricane base. Glue in place, then cover lightly with moss, securing with U-pins. Cut a 15" begonia branch and insert it into the left end of the foam. Insert a 10" branch on each side of it extending in the same direction. Insert another 10" branch to extend over the top of the 15" branch. Repeat on the other end to make an oblong base. Cut the rest of the branches to 5" and insert evenly in front of and behind the chimney, extending outward.

2 Cut a 9" sprig off each berry stem. Cut the remainder of each stem to 15" and insert one over each 15" begonia branch. Shape the berries and leaves to extend evenly among the begonia leaves. Cut one 9" into two 5" sprigs and insert into the foam front among the 5" begonia branches. Repeat in the back.

3 Cut the upper 9" off a sweet pea stem and insert over a 15" berry stem. Cut the rest of that stem into an 8", a 7" and a 6" sprig. Insert the 8" sprig behind and the 7" sprig in front of the 9" sweet pea. Insert the 6" sprig over the 9" sprig, angled slightly upward. Repeat on the other end. Cut the last stem into 4" sprigs and insert among the 5" begonia sprigs at similar angles.

4 Beginning at the left end of the arrangement, tuck and loop the ribbon through to the other end. Angle it to extend among the forward materials on the left end, in front of the hurricane, and among the materials on the back right side. Cut the silver king into 3"–5" sprigs and glue evenly spaced among all the materials. Insert the candle into the hurricane.

Fuchsia Topiary

20" tall vine topiary on a log base
2 yards of 1 ½" wide moss green taffeta wire-edged ribbon
1 ¾ yards of ¼" wide mauve twisted satin cord
2 stems of mauve silk fuchsias, each with four 1"–2" wide blossoms, 2 buds and many wired leaves
1 stem of burgundy/green silk grape leaves with 3 sprigs of four or five 2"–4" long leaves and brown stems with wired tendrils and moss
1 oz. of green preserved leatherleaf fern
1 oz. of naturally colored dried brisa maxima grass
½ oz. of green sheet moss
30-gauge wire
glue gun and sticks or tacky craft glue

1 Cut a fuchsia stem to 13". Wire it to curve from the bottom of the ball up the left side and over the top to the upper right. Cut the second fuchsia stem to 12". Place the stem end at the back and wrap the stem around the trunk, bringing it up the ball in front of the first stem; wire to secure.

2 Shape the grape leaves to curve naturally. Position the lowest leaves at the bottom of the ball and the rest to curve up among the fuchsias; wire to secure. Wrap the stem around the trunk and wire as inconspicuously as possible wherever necessary.

3 Use the ribbon to make a puffy bow (see page 20) with six 2½" loops, a 16" and a 20" tail. Glue to the bottom of the ball with the longer tail extending upward. Tuck and glue that tail among the flowers. Loosely wrap the shorter tail down the trunk, gluing as necessary. Use the cord to make a loopy bow (see page 21) with six 2"–3½" loops, a 10" and a 16" tail. Glue to the center of the first bow; allow the tails to drape.

4 Cut the fern into 5"–8" sprigs and glue evenly among the flowers and leaves, following similar angles. As shown above, cut 6"–9" brisa maxima sprigs and glue evenly spaced among all the materials, again at similar angles. Glue ½"–1" wide moss tufts evenly and sparingly over the ball and trunk to cover any exposed wires; also add tufts to the base.

Bundle from the Forest

12 oz. of 27"–32" long birch branches

2½" long mauve/brown mushroom bird

6 yards of jute twine

2 stems of peach/cream latex Japanese apricot blossoms, each with a 15" section of ⅜"–1" wide buds and blossoms

3 stems of green silk sprengeri, each with a 14" section of many 3"–5" sprigs

2 stems of green silk or PVC onion grass, each with thirty-six 12" blades

1 green latex fern with seven 8"–9" fronds and two curled fiddleheads

2 oz. of dark red preserved heather

1 oz. of green sheet moss

U-shaped floral pins

4"x2"x2" block of floral foam for silks

glue gun and sticks or tacky craft glue

1 Cut the twigs as needed, then bundle them. Do not place them all extending the same direction, but rather with fine twig ends extending at each end. Wrap the center twice, 1" apart, with wire to secure. Add more fine twigs to fill any empty areas. If you have curving twigs, put them on the right end, curving upward and back toward the center. Wrap jute over the wires and tie at the top, leaving 12" tails. Cut the foam to fit over the bundle center and glue

right of the jute. Cover the foam sides with moss, securing with U-pins.

2 Cut the fern stem to 1½" and insert into the foam center. Shape the leaves to curve naturally. Cut the stems (not the blades) of the onion grass to 1½" and insert them behind the fern. Cut one apricot stem to 16", curve the sprigs left, then insert into the right end. Cut the other stem into a 6", a 7" and a 9" sprig. Insert two in front of and one behind the first apricot stem, all curving naturally.

3 Cut the upper 9" off a sprengeri stem and insert among the apricot sprigs at the right. Cut the rest and one other sprengeri stem into 3- or 4-sprig sections and insert around the front, left and back foam, all angled away from the center.

4 Cut an 18" jute length and set aside. Use the rest to make a loopy bow (see page 21) with sixteen 2"–3" loops and 7"–14" tails; secure with the 18" length. Glue to the lower left front corner, angled as shown above. Cut the last sprengeri stem into 3"–4" sprigs and glue to fill empty spaces around the bottom of the foam. Cut the heather into 5"–12" sprigs and glue evenly spaced among all the materials as shown above. Glue the bird left of the bow, then glue moss tufts randomly among the twigs and around the bird.

Rose & Ivy Centerpiece

8" square by 2" deep granite-look florist's bowl

1¼ yards of 2½" wide tan/rose/green tapestry ribbon with rose wired edges

1 green silk grape ivy bush with nineteen 11"–14" long branches of 2"–3½" wide leaves

4 stems of dark yellow roses, each with four 1"–2½" wide blossoms, a bud and many wired latex leaves

1 branch of rust latex peaches with three 1¼"–2" peaches, green ⅜" berries, 4 white and 3 peach flowers and many leaves

two 9½"–10" naturally colored dried sunburst palm leaves

two 3"–4" naturally colored lotus pods on picks

two 3½" naturally colored dried protea blossoms on stems

two 2" giant acorns on picks

4 oz. of naturally colored dried chesta

1 oz. of green sheet moss

one U-shaped floral pin

4"x4"x3" block of floral foam for silks

glue gun and sticks or tacky craft glue

1 Round the corners of the foam top, then glue it into the bowl. Cover the sides with moss, securing with U-pins. Cut one 11" and five 14" ivy branches; insert three into the each side of the foam to extend down toward the table. Cut eight 11" branches; insert four evenly spaced across the foam front and four in the back. Cut the stems of the palms to 2", then insert as shown.

2 Cut all the rose stems to 12". Insert one into each long end, shaping the sprigs and leaves to extend naturally among the ivy leaves. Bend the bottom 2" of a rose stem at a right angle. Insert it into the right front corner of the foam extending left across the top and along the front. Turn the arrangement around and repeat on the back.

3 Cut off the upper 11" of the peach branch; insert into the foam center to extend right over the top. Cut the rest of the stem to 12" and repeat on the back. Cut each ribbon end in an inverted V. Beginning at one end of the arrangement, loop and tuck the ribbon throughout the materials and between the palm leaves to the other end; U-pin the center to keep it in place.

4 Cut the picks on the pods and the stems on the proteas to 2". Insert one of each in a cluster at the center front of the arrangement; repeat on the back. Cut the remaining ivy branches into 9" sprigs. Insert evenly spaced into the foam top as shown above. Cut the chesta into 9"–14" sprigs. Insert evenly spaced near materials of similar lengths following the same angles.

Cascade of Florals

crinkled papier-mâché boxes: one 7", one 8", one 9" wide

3 ½ yards of 2⅝" wide rust/green/tan printed ribbon

six 48" long strands of naturally colored raffia

6' green/rust silk fall ivy garland with 1 ¼"–2 ½" wide leaves

1 cream silk magnolia branch with four 2"–6" wide blossoms, a 1 ½" long bud and many leaves

1 stem of burgundy/red/green mini crabapples with three 8"–16" sprigs of ⅝"–¾" wide apples and many leaves

1 oz. of naturally colored dried Christina grass

½ oz. of green sheet moss

glossy cherry spray stain

2"x3"x4" block of floral foam for silks

glue gun and sticks or tacky craft glue

1 Stain the boxes and lids; do not paint the bottoms or insides, but be sure to stain the lid edges. To avoid runs, begin with a light coat, then repeat as necessary until the desired coverage is reached. Glue the lids on the boxes, then stack as shown and glue to secure. Cut the foam to fit around the top box and glue to the left side of the center box lid.

2 Cut the ivy into a 23", a 22", an 18" and four 6"–10" sprigs. Insert the 23" sprig into the foam front, curving down the boxes to the right. Insert the 22" sprig into the left side, curving forward, down and right. Insert the 18" sprig to the right of the first sprig, curving downward.

3 Cut the magnolia to 20". Insert it into the front extending over the 23" ivy sprig. Hold two raffia strands over the ribbon and handle as one. Make a puffy bow (see page 20) with a center loop, eight 3½" loops, a 34" and a 26" tail. Glue to the top extending over the left edge. Insert the remaining ivy sprigs evenly spaced over the top and back of the foam, curving one around the front and one around the back of the bow.

4 Cut the lowest sprig from the crabapple stem to 8". Insert it behind the magnolia beside the bow; curve it among the bow loops. Cut the rest of the stem to 18". Insert it right of the magnolia, following the same curves. Tuck the long ribbon tail down the front of the boxes and glue to hold. Tuck and glue the short tail down the left side. Cut the grass into 4"–11" sprigs and insert evenly spaced as shown in the large photo above. Glue moss tufts to cover any exposed foam.

Elegant Vase
of Flowers

All the stems will be held together and wired as you proceed; secure wire ends and add more wire as needed.

7" tall tulip-shaped clear glass vase

2¼ yards of 1½" wide bur- gundy taffeta wire-edged ribbon with a black sheen

2½ yards of ⅝" sheer gold ribbon with solid gold edges

12 oz. package of Everlasting Elegance™ clear floral arranging compound

5 stems of maroon silk peonies, each with a 5" wide blossom, a 1½" wide bud and many leaves

silk snapdragon stems: 2 stems of mauve/white and 1 stem of peach/yellow, each with a 16" section of ½"–2" long buds and blossoms plus many leaves

3 stems of white silk tulips, each with a 2½" tall blos- soms and 2 leaves

3 stems of creamy yellow silk bouvardia, each with three 3"–4" clusters of 1" wide blossoms and many leaves

4 stems of purple silk mini daisies, each with three 9"–12" sprigs of many ¾" wide blossoms and leaves

30-gauge green cloth-covered wire

1 Attach one end of a wire length to a mauve snapdragon over the lowest leaves on the stem.

2 Hold the snapdragon, a mini daisy and a peony together with the snapdragon and daisy extending about 4" above the peony blossom. Wrap the stems twice with the wire.

3 Turn the bouquet around. Add the peach snapdragon on the right side of the first stem, to extend 3" below it. Add a daisy stem on top to extend equally with the peach snapdragon; wire all the stems in place again.

4 Add the tulips to the bouquet, spacing them equal distances around the bouquet to extend 7" below the first snapdragon. Add the last snapdragon opposite from the peach one, extending 3" below the very first snapdragon. Wire.

5 Add the remaining four peonies, evenly spaced around the outside of the bouquet and positioned to extend 7" below the first snapdragon stem. Wire.

6 Add the bouvardia and the last mini daisy around the bouquet, spacing them evenly to extend just under the last peony blossoms. Wrap all the stems very securely with wire. Shape the sprigs to extend evenly amongst each other, angling outward from the center.

7 Hold the bouquet near the vase to determine how much of each stem to trim. Cut the excess stems off so the bouquet stands upright in the vase. Spread the stem ends apart so they look natural. Follow the manufacturer's instructions for mixing the arranging compound and pour into the vase. Carefully insert the bouquet into the compound, making sure it is straight. Leave the bouquet alone the correct amount of time—this is very important for success!

8 Hold the gold ribbon over the burgundy ribbon and handle as one. Tie them around the neck of the vase; trim excess. Make an oblong bow with a center loop, six 2¾"–3¼" loops, a 10" and a 15" tail. Glue the bow over the knot.

Dried Flowers with Flair

Delicate and sometimes fragrant, many dried flowers lend an old-fashioned appeal to floral arrangements. In fact, Victorians used dried flowers to decorate their homes. Today, the dried materials available to us include not only flowers but also twigs, grasses, leaves, pods, vegetables and fruits. Rich with varying textures, these materials are an important addition to most arrangements and decorations.

Dried grasses and pods provide a natural, garden or woodsy look to designs; baby's breath, caspia and German statice are great filler flowers, eliminating empty spaces within an arrangement. Many dried materials in stores are already painted or dyed in decorator colors. Using them adds more color than usually found in drieds. Dyed dark green leaves add a fresher look to a design than plain dried leaves do.

Often silk arrangements need the addition of dried materials to make them look more realistic. Most pieces in this book have drieds as part of the design; this section, however, includes designs made just from dried materials. Pages 100–103 feature an identification guide for the dried flowers and

aristea

artichoke

avena

baby's breath

barley or wheat

bell cup

bell reed

leatherleaf fern

materials used in this book. They are placed in alphabetical order, beginning at the upper left and rotating clockwise around the first two pages, then continuing in the same manner on the next pages. Dried materials are fun to work with and easy to handle.

Flowers and plants can be air-dried naturally, kiln-dried (which preserves more of the color), freeze-dried or processed with a desiccant such as silica gel. Glycerin-preserved materials can be recognized by their fresher feel, softness and pliability.

Before removing very delicate dried materials from their cellophane wrapping, hold the bunch over steam for a minute (be very careful that the steam doesn't burn you). The steam will soften the flowers and stems a bit, allowing them to be pulled apart more easily without shattering. A light steaming can also enhance the appearance of many dried flowers, fluffing and refreshing leaves and blossoms or opening buds. Another option for conditioning drieds before use is to mist them lightly with water.

lavender

larkspur

koolseed

isolepsis grass

heather

happy flowers

gypsophila

hairy pod (or fiber ball)

German statice

giant acorn

billy buttons

birch branches

bloom broom

brisa maxima

brisa media

bromus secalinus grass

buck foliage

bupleurum

canella pods

cedar

If the stems of dried flowers and grasses bend or break when you try to insert them into foam, wire a wood pick to the stem bottom—be sure to insert the pick far enough into the foam so all you can see is the flower stem.

Properly cared for, dried arrangements are very long-lasting. Display them out of direct sunlight, which will fade the blooms. A too-humid environment will cause the materials to droop, but insufficient humidity or high temperatures will make them over-dry, brittle and fragile.

Whether you dry the flowers yourself or buy some of the many types available in stores, dried flowers and materials are a pleasure to work with and add warmth to any floral design!

Christina grass

eucalyptus

centaurca

chili pepper stem

chesta

curly ting ting

chili pepper

floral buttons

lemon
leaf

lotus pod

maiden
fern

maidenhair
fern

linum
atraxa

statice
sinuata

liatris

lino
grass

tarwe

starflowers

stirlingia

star
cone

starburst

sunburst
palm leaf

sprengeri

rice grass

sponge
mushroom

salal leaves

sabulosum

roses

silver
king

silene grass

safflowers

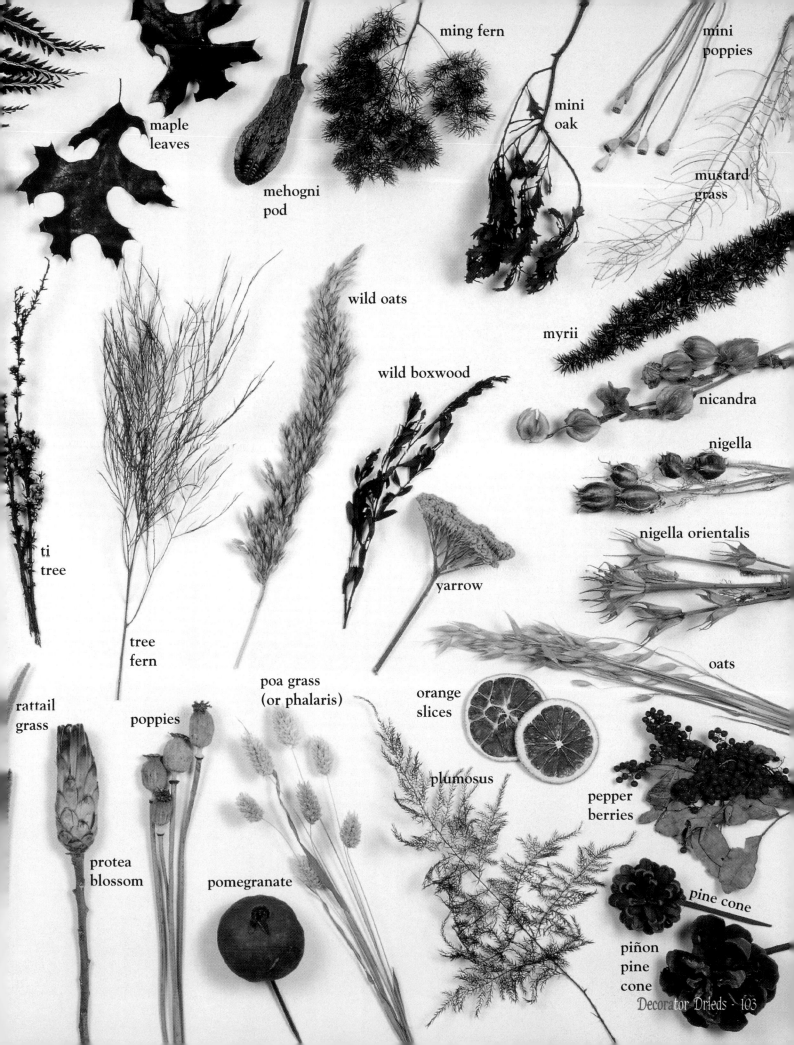

maple
leaves

ming fern

mini
poppies

mini
oak

mehogni
pod

mustard
grass

wild oats

myrii

wild boxwood

nicandra

nigella

nigella orientalis

ti
tree

yarrow

tree
fern

oats

poa grass
(or phalaris)

orange
slices

rattail
grass

poppies

plumosus

pepper
berries

protea
blossom

pomegranate

pine cone

piñon
pine
cone

10"x5" bleached willow basket with a 6" tall handle

1½ yards of 2⅝" wide metallic gold/ivory ribbon

6 oz. of white dried ti tree branches

6 oz. of light green dried oats or avena

3 oz. of light green lino grass

3 oz. of white dried starflowers

2 oz. of naturally colored dried rice grass

2 oz. of naturally colored dried poa grass or phalaris

4 oz. of naturally colored dried nicandra

2 oz. of gray American Moss® excelsior

three 8"x4"x3" blocks of floral foam for drieds

U-shaped floral pins

3" wired wood picks

24-gauge wire

glue gun and sticks or tacky craft glue

1 Cut the foam blocks to fit into the basket with 1½" extending above the rim. Glue in place, inserting pieces around the edges to fill empty spaces. Cut two 13" ti tree sprigs; insert one on each side of the handle. Cut ten 9" and eleven 11" ti tree sprigs. Insert the 9" sprigs around the rim, extending parallel with the tabletop. Insert the 11" sprigs between the 13" and 9" sprigs, angled as shown.

2 Hold 8–10 starflower stems together at varying heights. Wire to a pick, making a 12" "stem." Repeat; insert one near each 13" ti tree sprig. Cut and pick the remaining starflowers to 8"–10". Insert evenly spaced near ti tree sprigs of similar lengths, matching the angles.

3 Cut the avena into 9"–13" sprigs and insert evenly spaced near materials of similar lengths. Repeat with the lino and poa grass. Cut the rice grass into 10"–14" sprigs and insert as for the previous materials, using wood picks as needed.

4 Cut the nicandra into 10"–12" sprigs. Insert among the 11" and 13" sprigs of other materials. Carefully tuck moss around the stems to cover any exposed foam, securing with U-pins. Use the ribbon to make a puffy bow (see page 20) with a center loop, four 3½" loops and 8" tails. Attach to a pick and insert into the foam next to one handle base.

Bird's Nest Basket

6"x3" mossy basket
   with a 5" handle
one 5½" long
   blue/black
   feathered bird
three 40" strands of
   natural raffia
1 oz. of 12"–18"
   long natural-
   colored dried
   birch branches
1 oz. of green
   preserved
   plumosus
1 oz. of natural-
   colored dried
   silene grass
½ oz. of naturally
   colored dried
   centaurea
1 oz. of green
   sheet moss
3"x2"x3" block
   of floral foam
   for drieds
glue gun and
   sticks or tacky
   craft glue

1 Cut the floral foam to fit against one inner side of the basket near the left end of the handle; glue in place. Cover with moss, then put more moss in the right side of the basket to make a "nest" for the bird. Cut fifteen 7"–14" birch twigs. Insert into the foam angled toward the inside of the basket, positioning longer twigs near the outer edge and shorter ones nearer the center.

2 Cut the centaurea into 6"–11" sprigs. Insert them evenly spaced near twigs of similar lengths, angled toward the inside of the basket. Repeat with the silene.

3 Cut two 6" plumosus sprigs. Glue one to extend from the basket handle on the left around the front rim and the other to extend from the same spot around the back rim. Cut the remaining plumosus into 5"–11" sprigs and glue them evenly among all the materials.

4 Glue the bird into the nest near the basket front rim. Set aside one raffia strand. Hold the others together to make a raffia loopy bow (see page 119) with 2½" loops and 15" tails. Glue to the front handle base on the left side.

Bundles of Bouquets

13"x11" oval grapevine wreath
7 stems of red dried roses
1 oz. of naturally colored dried nigella orientalis
1 oz. of light green dried rattail grass
1 oz. of naturally colored dried happy flowers
2 oz. of green preserved myrii
two 3" wide naturally colored dried orange
    slices
one 2" wide naturally colored bell pod
one 2" tall piñon pine cone
one 3" long mehogni pod on a pick
30-gauge wire
glue gun and sticks or tacky craft glue

1 **To make each bundle:** Hold the materials at varying heights, positioning them with no empty spaces among the heads. Measure to the length listed below and wire ½" above that point. Trim to even the stems below the wire and glue the bundle in place on the wreath.

2 Make a bundle of 8"–13" nigella orientalis sprigs. Glue this bundle on the left side of the wreath, extending upward beyond the wreath top. Make a 7"–11" bundle of the rattail grass and glue left of the orientalis.

3 Bundle the roses 5"–8" long. Glue them over the nigella orientalis. Bundle the myrii 5"–10" long; glue right of the roses. Bundle the happy flowers 3"–7" long; glue left of the roses over the rattail grass.

4 Trim away ¼ of each orange slice. Glue one slice below right of the stem bottoms, angling from upper right to lower left. Glue the second slice below and slightly forward of the first, shifting the angle. Cut the picks off the pods and cone. Glue in a cluster over the bundle stems as shown. Attach a wire loop hanger to the upper wreath back (see page 12).

Embellished Heart Box

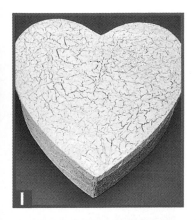

7 ½"x7 ½"x3" heart-shaped papier-mâché box with a crinkled finish
1 ¾"x2" brass heart charm with an open center
acrylic paints: dusty purple, antique white
crackle medium, dark walnut acrylic stain, matte acrylic spray sealer
1 ¼ yards of 1 ⅝" wide dark burgundy taffeta wire-edged ribbon
1 ¼ yards of ⅝" wide antique gold wired braid
5 stems of pink dried roses
½ oz. of dark green preserved plumosus
½ oz. of naturally colored dried rice grass
1" wide paintbrush, container for water, clean cloths, glue gun and sticks or tacky craft glue

1 Paint the box and lid purple; let dry. Follow the manufacturer's directions to apply crackle medium and white paint over the purple; the paint should crackle as it dries. Spray sealer over the box and lid. Let dry, then use a cloth to rub walnut stain lightly over the box and lid; wipe off to the desired darkness. Spray again with sealer.

2 Cut a 12" length each of ribbon and braid. Glue the ribbon diagonally across the lid from the upper right to the lower left; glue the ends inside the lid. Glue the braid over the ribbon. Hold the remaining braid over the remaining ribbon and handle as one to make a puffy bow (see page 20) with four 2½" loops and 5" tails. Glue the bow to the upper right of the box over the ribbon.

3 To antique the charm, paint it black and wipe most of the paint off before it dries. Spray with sealer and let dry, then glue into the bow center angled as shown. Cut four roses to 2". Glue one into the bow center angled back toward the upper right lid edge. Glue one on the right side of the charm, angled over the lower bow loops. Glue one into the bow center angled over the lower left loop. Cut a rose to 3" and glue extending forward from under the heart with the last 2" rose above it.

4 Cut the plumosus and rice grass into 2"–4½" sprigs. Glue evenly spaced among the roses and bow loops at similar angles as shown in the large photo above.

Dried Garden Wreath

22" round TWIGS™ woven wreath
3 yards of 2¼" wide green ribbon with gold wired edges
2 oz. (6 stems) of dark green dried maiden fern
4 oz. of yellow dried yarrow
5 oz. of naturally colored dried nigella orientalis
2 oz. of green dried silene grass
3 oz. of naturally colored dried floral buttons
2 oz. of naturally colored dried rice grass
24-gauge wire
glue gun and sticks or tacky craft glue

1 Cut half the fern into 12"–15" sprigs. Glue to the wreath extending down each side from the center top, leaving about 8" open at the center bottom. Allow 2½"–3" of the outer wreath edge to show. Set aside the rest of the fern for step 4.

2 Use the ribbon to make a puffy bow (see page 20) with a center loop, eight 3½" loops, a 10" and a 14" tail. Glue the bow to the center top over the fern stems with the tails draping through the wreath center.

3 Cut the yarrow into 4"–5" sprigs. Glue them to the wreath evenly spaced on each side following the angles of the fern sprigs. Cut the nigella orientalis, silene and floral buttons into 3"–5" sprigs. Glue the orientalis and silene evenly spaced among the fern and yarrow. Glue the floral buttons in clusters of three evenly spaced among the fern and yarrow.

4 Cut the remaining fern into 5"–8" sprigs and glue evenly to fill empty spaces and bring the green color forward among the other colors. Cut the rice grass into 6"–10" sprigs and glue evenly for a lacy look. Attach a wire loop hanger to the upper back (see page 12).

Topiary from the Garden

4" tall terra cotta pot with saucer
2 yards of ¼" wide mauve twisted satin cord
2 yards of ⅛" wide dark green satin ribbon
4 oz. of green preserved ming fern
5 oz. of pink dried ti tree branches
4 oz. of white dried starflowers
2 oz. of light green dried silene grass
1 oz. of green sheet moss
4½" ball of floral foam for drieds and silks
21" length of ¾" wide wood dowel
3–4 cups of patching plaster
disposable container for mixing, water
2½" wired wood picks, 24-gauge wire
glue gun and sticks or tacky craft glue

1 Insert the dowel ½" into one side of the foam as shown in the drawing above. Remove it and use a knife to dig out the excess foam to make the hole 1" deep. Apply glue to the dowel end and reinsert. Glue the pot to the saucer. Mix the plaster with water to a very thick consistency. Pour into the pot, then insert the dowel into the plaster. Brace it to stand straight, let the plaster harden.

2 Cut the fern into 5½"–7½" sprigs. To eliminate bent stems, insert each stem into the ball, remove it, then apply glue to the stem end and reinsert. Insert two of the longest sprigs next to the dowel to extend downward. Insert the rest to evenly cover the ball, spacing shorter sprigs among longer ones.

3 Hold 8–12 starflowers together at varying heights; cut them to 5"–7" and attach to a wood pick. Insert into the foam. Repeat evenly over the ball. Cut the ti tree into 6"–8" sprigs and the silene into 5"–7" sprigs. Insert as for the fern and starflowers.

4 Handle the cord and ribbon as one to make a loopy bow (see page 20) with two 4" and two 6" loops, a 13" and a 16" tail. Attach to a pick and insert next to the dowel to extend downward. Fill the pot with moss. Tuck small moss tufts among the materials on the ball if necessary to hide any exposed foam.

Gathering Bouquet

2 oz. (3 branches) of dark green preserved salal leaves
2 oz. of purple preserved statice sinuata
2 oz. of pink dried larkspur
2 oz. of naturally colored dried floral buttons
3 stems of naturally colored dried protea flowers, each with a
   3½" long unopened head
1 oz. of naturally colored dried brisa media grass
2⅓ yards of 2⅝" wide tan/green/mauve print hopsack ribbon
30-gauge wire
glue gun and sticks or tacky craft glue

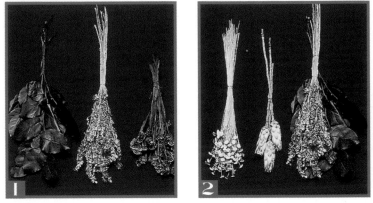

1 Hold the salal branches together with the center branch extending a little farther than the side ones. Wire in two places to secure. Set aside two larkspur stems for step 4. Hold the rest together, pulling up the center stems above the side stems. Wire to secure. Repeat with the statice, again saving two stems for step 4.

2 Hold the floral button stems together at varying heights, making a 6" long section of flower heads. Wire to secure. Hold the protea stems together with one extending further than the others as shown; wire. Wire the larkspur bundle over the left side of the salal, almost to the ends of the leaves.

3 Place the statice right of the larkspur with the blossom ends extending to within 3" of the salal leaf ends. Place the floral button bundle above left of the statice; wire to secure both bundles. Wire the protea bundle right of the floral button bundle.

4 Wrap and glue a 3" ribbon length over the exposed wires. Use the remaining ribbon to make an oblong bow (see page 20) with a center loop, four 2½"–3½" loops, a 7" and a 12" tail. Wire to the bouquet stems just above the protea blossoms, angled left, then twist the wire into a loop hanger at the upper back (see page 12). Apply glue under the bow to keep it from twisting on the bouquet front. Loop and glue the tails among the materials. Cut off excess stems, leaving about 3"–4" extending

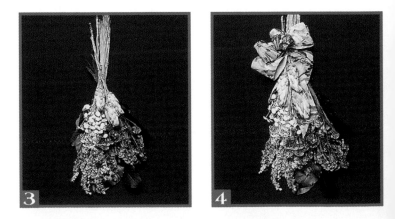

unevenly above the bow. Cut the remaining larkspur and statice to 3". Glue to fill any empty spaces in the larkspur bundle. Cut the brisa media into 3"–5" sprigs. Glue evenly spaced between the bundles.

Harvest of Wheat & Driels

2½ yards of 1½" wide rust/green/orange tapestry
    ribbon
1 oz. of naturally colored raffia
8 oz. of naturally colored dried bearded wheat
    or barley
3 stems of red-orange dried protea, each with a
    5"–6" blossom head
3 oz. of natural dried star cone stems (about
    6 blossoms)
3 oz. of naturally colored dried lino grass
3 oz. of naturally colored dried chili pepper stems
30-gauge wire
glue gun and sticks or tacky craft glue

1 Hold all the wheat together just under the heads. By pulling the back heads upward, arrange to form an 11"x12" oval. Wire under the lowest heads. Insert the protea stems into the bundle as shown.

2 Cut an 8" ribbon length; place five raffia strands over the ribbon and handle as one. Wrap them around the bouquet over the wire. Knot in front to secure; trim the ribbon tails. Hold three raffia strands over the remaining ribbon and handle together to make an oblong bow (see page 20) with a center loop, two 3" and four 3½" loops, and 15" tails. Glue the bow over the knot at the bouquet front.

3 Trim the star cone blossoms to 7"–11" and glue evenly spaced around the protea. Repeat with the chilies, gluing them evenly among all the materials and placing several to curve over the front and sides of the bundle. Glue two or three peppers to extend above and below the bow center.

4 Cut the lino into 7"–9" sprigs and glue evenly spaced among the wheat. Position some to extend outward at the sides of the bundle. At the back, insert a wire into the bundle and bring forward around the ribbon. Twist the wire into a loop hanger (see page 12).

Hats Off!

18" wide wicker hat
2½ yards of 2½" wide sheer burgundy floral print ribbon
7½ yards of 6" wide cream tulle
4 oz. of pink dried ti tree branches
3 oz. of dark green dried bloom broom
3 oz. of naturally colored dried oats
30-gauge wire
glue gun and sticks or tacky craft glue

1 Cut three 36" tulle lengths. Hold together and pinch one end; wire to secure. Measure 5", pinch and wire; repeat to the end. Glue one wired end to the hat near the crown (this will be the back). Wrap the length around the hat, gluing the wired areas to the crown every 4". Overlap the ends and trim excess.

2 Cut the remaining tulle into three 54" lengths, hold together and handle as one. Make a collar bow (see page 18) with 4" loops and 15"–16" tails. Glue over the tulle ends at the hat back. Use the burgundy ribbon to make an oblong bow (see page 20) with a center loop, two 2½" and four 3½" loops, and 14"–15" tails. Glue to the center of the tulle bow.

3 Cut the bloom broom into 3"–4" sprigs. Glue around the crown, tucking the stems under the tulle edges and folds. Cut 5"–6" sprigs and glue to extend out and downward from under the bow centers.

4 Cut the ti tree into 4"–5" sprigs. Glue evenly spaced among the bloom broom. Glue 6"–7" sprigs extending downward from under the bows. Cut the oats into 3"–5" sprigs and glue evenly spaced among all the flowers as shown in the large photo. Attach a wire loop hanger to the upper back (see page 12).

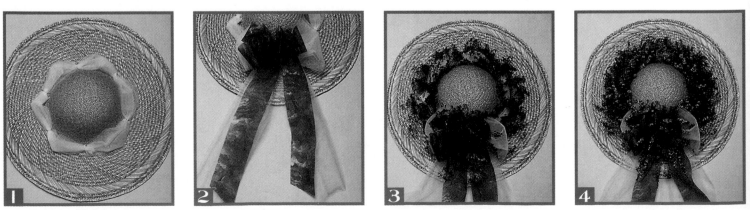

A Full House

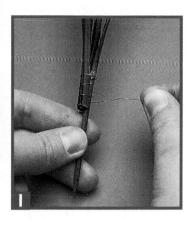

8"x9"x6" house-shaped log basket with a 7"
  tall handle
12 stems of yellow dried billy buttons
three 33" stems of naturally colored dried
  aristea
2 oz. of dark green preserved isolepsis grass

2 oz. of green preserved leatherleaf fern
2 oz. of naturally colored dried rice grass
½ oz. of green sheet moss
3" long wired wood picks
4"x3"x3" block of floral foam for drieds
glue gun and sticks or tacky craft glue

1 Trim the foam to fit one end of the basket and glue into the right side. Glue moss to cover the foam. Hold two 17" grass sprigs (there are multiple strands on each sprig) together and wire to a wood pick. Insert into the foam at the center right.

2 Repeat, making nine more 10"–17" grass picks. (Since the sprigs start out 17" long, make shorter sprigs by holding two together and cutting to the desired length before wiring them to the pick.) Insert evenly spaced with the long ones at the right, the medium stems in the center and the shortest on the left side.

3 Cut the billy buttons to 8"–13" sprigs. Insert a 13" sprig into the foam center with a 12" sprig in front and one behind. Insert an 11" sprig on each side of the 13" sprig and the shorter sprigs around the foam sides. Angle all the sprigs away from the 13" one. Cut the aristea into six 8"–15" sprigs. Insert them evenly among the billy buttons at similar angles, with the shorter sprigs around the left edge.

4 Cut the fern into 4"–10" sprigs. Attach each to a wood pick and insert evenly spaced with longer ones in the center and shorter ones around the front, back and left edges. Cut the rice grass into 8"–16" sprigs; insert near isolepsis stems of similar lengths as shown in the large photo. Cover any exposed foam with moss.

Root Wreath
Filled with Drieds

28" wide root wreath
4 oz. of light green dried lemon leaf
 branches
12 stems of dark burgundy dried
 roses
2 oz. of naturally colored dried
 nigella
6 stems of pink dried liatris
2 oz. of naturally colored dried
 starburst
6 oz. of light green dried avena or
 oats
30-gauge wire
glue gun and sticks or tacky craft
 glue

1 Attach a wire loop hanger to the wreath back (see page 12). Cut all but two lemon leaf branches into sprigs of 2–4 leaves. Glue evenly spaced around the inner edge, angling clockwise, with some extending toward the outside.

2 Cut four rose stems to 3"–4", hold together at varying heights and glue in a cluster among the lemon leaves. Repeat for two more clusters; glue evenly spaced around the wreath following the angles of the lemon leaves.

3 Make two liatris bundles as in step 2, but use three blossoms with 1"–2" stems for each. Glue the clusters opposite each other on the wreath. Repeat with the starburst, using five stems for each cluster and making six clusters; glue evenly around the wreath.

4 Divide the nigella sprigs into clusters of five and glue evenly spaced around the wreath. Cut the avena into 5"–7" sprigs. Glue sprigs evenly spaced to fill any empty areas as shown above. Cut the remaining lemon leaves off the stems and glue extending forward among all the materials.

Wreath of Fallen Leaves

15" wide straw wreath
3¾ yards of 1⅜" wide
   rust/brown/green print ribbon
2 oz. of naturally colored raffia
8 oz. of brown preserved maple leaves
6 oz. of red preserved maple leaves
5 oz. of yellow preserved eucalyptus
4 oz. of green preserved wild boxwood
U-shaped floral pins
glue gun and sticks or tacky craft glue

1 To make a hanger, bend the ends of one U-pin back at a 45° angle. Insert the ends into the wreath back with the loop toward the upper edge. Apply glue around the hanger to secure it.

2 Cut the brown leaf branches into sprigs of 3–4 leaves. Place a sprig extending clockwise on the wreath front; insert a U-pin over the sprig securely into the wreath—if it has a tendency to spring back out, glue the pin in place before inserting. Repeat with the remaining brown leaf sprigs, loosely covering the wreath, with some around the outside and inside.

3 Repeat step 2 with the red leaves, placing them evenly among the brown ones. Cut the boxwood and eucalyptus into 5"–7" sprigs. U-pin them equally spaced among the previous leaves, tucking the stems underneath to hide them and the U-pins.

4 Cut the ribbon into 15" lengths. Hold a raffia strand over a ribbon length and handle as one to make into a 4" loop with a 6" tail extending upward behind the loop. Secure with wire, then trim away excess raffia. Repeat for nine more loops, then glue them evenly spaced around the wreath, following the same angles as the leaf sprigs. Use each remaining raffia strand to make a set of 4" loops with 6"–9" tails (see page 119); use your fingernail to shred the loops and tails. Glue evenly spaced around the wreath.

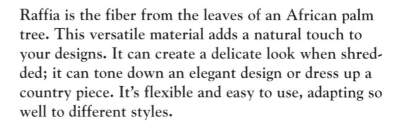

Raffia to Rave About

Raffia is the fiber from the leaves of an African palm tree. This versatile material adds a natural touch to your designs. It can create a delicate look when shredded; it can tone down an elegant design or dress up a country piece. It's flexible and easy to use, adapting so well to different styles.

In craft stores raffia can be purchased either dried or preserved with glycerine. Either works well; preserved raffia is softer and more pliable, yet strong. Dried raffia breaks more easily when stressed, such as when it's knotted, but it adds a wonderful look to any design.

Because it's so inexpensive, you can keep it on hand to use whenever a design needs a special touch. Since there are many strands in a hank—and it can be shredded into finer strands—one package lasts through several arrangements.

Raffia is available in decorator colors, including black and orange for Halloween or red and green for Christmas. If you can't find it in just the right color, you can dye it yourself. Use a liquid fabric dye found in grocery stores. In a clean container, dilute ¼ cup dye in 1½ gallons of very hot water. Immerse the bundle of raffia into the prepared dye and stir it with a clean stick (a new paint stick works great!) until the desired color is achieved. Be sure to use an old container, as it might be dyed too. Remove the raffia,

let it drain until it can be easily handled, then hang it to air dry. Place newspapers under the bundle to catch any drips. As it dries, turn it and pull inner strands to the outside. The raffia is ready to use as soon as it is dry.

However you use raffia, whether it be to make a decorative doll, a bouquet or a wall decoration, this natural fiber enhances nearly any design and style.

Tips for Success:

To avoid accidentally breaking a dried raffia strand when tying a bow or bouquet, first soak it for a minute in water, then blot dry. (only the tying strand needs to be wet, not all the strands). This makes it strong enough to tie without breaking.

Split or shred the raffia if a finer, more delicate look is needed. To shred a long strand of raffia, begin at one end and split it with your thumbnail; tear the strand carefully to the other end. Repeat as many times as desired with each strand to make it as narrow as needed. To shred strands for a bow, carefully split the loops into fine strands and tear them down to the binding wire; repeat with each loop. Shred the bow tails by splitting them at the end, then tearing each strand back to the wire.

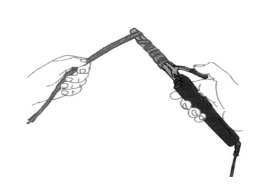

Curly raffia strands have a nice ripple and add interest to any design in which that curl can be preserved. It's not as readily available as regular raffia, but nearly the same look can be duplicated with a curling iron. Set the iron on high and wrap the strands onto it as you would to curl hair. Remember raffia is a dried leaf; use caution when heating it, as it will burn. It doesn't take long for the curl to set, so begin with short times until you know just how curly you want the raffia.

Ribbon Loop with Raffia

Adding Raffia to a Ribbon Bow or Loop:

Raffia can add a natural look to a ribbon bow. Place one or two strands over the ribbon and hold together while making the bow. Depending on the number and size of loops, you may come to the end of the raffia before the end of the ribbon. In that case, allow the end to extend away from the bow as an extra tail. Then add a new strand over the top of the ribbon and continue to the end of the bow. When the bow loops are done and you're bringing the ribbon end up to make the loop for tails, more raffia can be added if desired; position the centers of the strands under the bow center and wire them all together.

Puffy Bow with Raffia

Raffia Loopy Bow:

1 Measure the desired tail length from one end of a raffia strand, then make a loop on each side of your thumb.

2 Continue to loop the raffia strand back and forth until all the raffia is used. Wire to secure, or tie the center with another strand of raffia and knot it at the back.

Raffia Collar Bow:

Hold 20–30 raffia strands together and form them into a circle, crossing the ends at the bottom. Pinch together, forming a bow, and adjust the loop sizes and tail lengths. Tie the center with a raffia strand; knot it at the back. Blend the ends into the other tails.

Raffia Loops:

Hold the specified number of strands together. Measure the desired tail length from one end and hold the strands together at that point. Fold the strands above your hand, making a loop of the specified length, and repeat until all the raffia is used. Wire at the base of the loop, turning the tails upward or letting them hang as indicated in the project.

- 16"x7" round rattan basket with an 11" tall handle
- 2 oz. of naturally colored raffia
- 2 oz. of purple raffia
- 2½ yards of 2⅝" wide purple abaca ribbon
- 3 stems of pale purple silk hollyhocks, each with seven 2" wide blossoms and many leaves
- 2 stems of purple/green berries, each with two 7"–10" branches of ⅜" wide berries and brown leaves
- 6 oz. of pink preserved ti tree branches
- 4 oz. of naturally colored dried rice grass
- 30-gauge wire
- glue gun and sticks or tacky craft glue

1 Hold together five strands of purple and three strands of natural raffia; wire 2" from one end. Shred the strands to 1/16"–1/8" wide with your fingernail. Wire the strands together every 11"; trim excess. Repeat for another garland. Wire one end of a garland at one handle base. Loop and glue the wired areas of the garland below the basket rim every 8". Attach the second garland over the end of the first and continue back to the starting point; trim excess. Fold four strands of each color in half and wire ½" from the fold. Shred the strands, then wire the folded end over the garland at the handle base. Wrap the ends of this bundle up the handle, wiring in two places to secure the wraps.

2 Hold a hollyhock and a berry stem together; shape the sprigs to intersperse. Wire the stems together and trim to 15". Wire three 15"–17" ti tree and ten 12"–18" rice grass stems among the flowers. Wire this cluster to the handle base at an angle as shown. Glue more rice grass and ti tree sprigs as needed to fill empty spaces.

3 Hold two raffia strands over the ribbon and handle as one to make a puffy bow (see page 20) with a center loop, eight 3¾" loops, an 8" and a 10" tail. Glue the bow over the wires on the flower cluster at the handle base. Shred more purple and natural raffia strands. Hold two 1/16" wide strands of each color together and make a raffia loopy bow (see page 119) with 2" loops and 6"–10" tails. Repeat for four more bows.

4 Cut ten 2" long hollyhocks off the stems. Pull off ten hollyhock leaves. Cut 15–18 ti tree sprigs to 2"–3" long and the remaining rice grass into 3"–4" sprigs. Cut a berry stem into five 5-berry sprigs. At each wired point, glue a berry sprig and two hollyhocks with a leaf on each side. Glue three ti tree and three rice grass sprigs among the hollyhocks. Glue a raffia loopy bow below each of these clusters.

Raffia Arch & Birdhouse

20" long wire arch form
5"x5"x4" wood birdhouse with an eye screw hanger
3" long peach/blue mushroom bird
3¾ yards of 1⅜" wide terra cotta printed moiré ribbon
8 oz. of naturally colored raffia
3 stems of coral/cream silk roses, each with 3 sprigs of
    six ¾"–1¾" wide blossoms and wired leaves
1 green silk piggyback plant with 8 branches of 1"–2"
    wide leaves
7 oz. of brown dried stirlingia
acrylic paints: light terra cotta, cream, brown
½" wide paintbrush, water container
clean cloth, sandpaper, matte acrylic spray varnish
30-gauge wire
glue gun and sticks or tacky craft glue

1 Separate the raffia into five equal bunches and temporarily secure each with wire. Hold the ends of one bunch even, then fold the ends down to make a 5" loop. Secure with wire, then cut the loop off, holding the remaining raffia together. Make another 5" loop with the rest of the strands. Repeat with three more bunches for a total of eight loops. Remove and set aside ten raffia strands from the last bunch, then make a 5" loop with the rest. Place a loop between one set of prongs on the wire form and secure. Repeat with seven more loops, then glue the last one at the top extending upward.

2 Sand the house and wipe clean. Paint the roof and perch terra cotta, the walls cream and the base brown. Let dry; varnish. Screw the eye into the roof peak, slightly to the back. Glue the bird to the perch. Thread a thick raffia strand through the eye, then tie it to the arch center to extend 2" below the form.

3 Cut 4"–5" rose sprigs off the stems. Cut the piggyback branches to 5". Hold a rose sprig over a piggyback branch and glue together over the lowest raffia loop on the left side. Repeat on each raffia loop, then glue the last rose sprig over the center loops, extending upward. Cut the stirlingia into 6"–8" sprigs. Glue them evenly spaced near the rose sprigs and at similar angles.

4 Use the ribbon to make an oblong bow (see page 20) with no center loop, twelve 2½"–4" loops and 23" tails. Glue to the arch center at an angle as shown. Hold nine raffia strands together to make a collar bow with 3" loops; tie with the last strand. Glue this bow over the ribbon bow. Drape one ribbon and half the raffia tails to the left side and glue among the raffia loops. Glue any leftover rose leaves around the bow loops. Make a wire loop hanger (see page 12) at the center back.

Braid Filled with Flowers

8 oz. of naturally colored raffia, tied together at one end
4 yards of 2" wide red very sheer ribbon with gold edges
4 stems of pink/cream silk roses, each with two 2½" wide blossoms and many leaves
3 stems of golden cream silk tweedia, each with four 9" sprigs of many 1½" wide blossoms
6 stems of dark brown dried pods, each with sprigs of two or three 1½" long pods
3 oz. of green preserved sprengeri
24-gauge wire
glue gun and sticks or tacky craft glue

1 Wrap wire around the tied end of the raffia, twist the ends together at the back, then twist them into a loop for a hanger. Hang the raffia on a secure hook and braid it. (To braid: Separate the raffia into three equal bunches. Bring the right bunch over the center bunch, then bring the left bunch over the center bunch. Repeat.) When the braid is 21" long, wrap wire around the loose ends to secure it.

2 Use the ribbon to make a puffy bow (see page 20) with a center loop, eight 4" loops and 28"–30" tails. Wire and glue it over the wired area on the upper end of the braid. Cut 3" rose sprigs off the stems; cut off all the leaf sprigs. Glue a rose above the bow, one below it angled right, and the rest evenly spaced along the braid. Glue a leaf sprig near each rose and the rest evenly spaced along the edges, angled outward and down.

3 Cut 3"–4" tweedia sprigs off the stem. Glue one on each side of the rose above the bow, two on each side of the bow and the rest evenly spaced along the braid, angled downward and outward. Cut the sprengeri into 4"–5" sprigs. Glue them along the outer edges of the braid and evenly spaced among the flowers. Glue 2"–3" sprengeri sprigs among the bow loops.

4 Cut 3" pod sprigs off the main stem. Glue them evenly spaced among all the materials. Loop a bow tail down one side of the braid and tuck it in, gluing to secure. Repeat on the other side.

Crocheted Hearts with Rosebuds

ecru crocheted heart wreaths: one 6", one 10"
1¼ yards of ¼" wide mauve satin ribbon
six 50" strands of sage green raffia
*2 stems of pink silk rosebuds, each with 5 sprigs
    of 3–6 buds, ⅝" long, and many sage green
    leaves*
1 oz. of naturally colored dried rice grass
1 oz. of mauve dried pepper berries
30-gauge wire
glue gun and sticks or tacky craft glue

1 Glue the small heart over the lower right of the large one, angled as shown. Set aside two raffia strands. Hold the rest together and make a raffia collar bow (see page 119) with 2" loops and 30"–36" tails. Secure with the last strand, then shred all the loops and tails. Use the ribbon to make a loopy bow (see page 21) with six 1½" loops, a 16" and a 9" tail. Glue it to the center of the raffia bow with the short tail extending left.

2 Glue both bows to the right shoulder of the large heart. On the left tails, measure 7" from the bow center. Knot the ribbon tail around the raffia tails. Repeat on the right tails, 12" from the bow. Bring the left tails to the left shoulder of the large heart and glue to secure. Bring the right tails downward, behind the small wreath's right shoulder, then through the wreath center. Glue the knot at the point.

3 Cut two 6-blossom, 3¼" long rose sprigs and glue one to extend from under the bow loops on each side. Cut six ½"–1" rosebuds; glue in a cluster above and in the bow center. Glue three 1"–2" rosebuds to the each shoulder of the small heart. Glue another 1" rosebud extending forward from the center of the heart.

4 Use a 24" long ¹⁄₁₆" wide raffia strand to make a set of three 1½" loops with 2" tails (see page 119). Repeat with another strand, then glue one among the rosebuds on each side of the small heart. Cut 1"–3" sprigs of pepper berries and glue evenly spaced among the rosebuds, following the same angles. Repeat with 2"–4" rice grass sprigs. Fill empty spaces with leftover rosebuds. Attach a wire loop hanger to the upper back (see page 12).

Autumn Topiary

31" tall vine
topiary
3 yards of 2⅝"
wide brown/rust
sheer ribbon
16 strands of
naturally col-
ored raffia
9' long rust/green
silk ivy garland
with ⅞"–2¾"
wide leaves
2 oz. of green
preserved
plumosus
3 oz. of naturally
colored dried
safflowers
3 oz. of naturally
colored dried
linum atraxa
3 oz. of gold
preserved
eucalyptus
30-gauge wire
glue gun and sticks
or tacky craft
glue

1 Cut the excess stem off each end of the garland. Hook or wire one end at the base, then wrap the vine up the trunk. Be sure the sprigs extend upward as though growing up the tree. Wire the vine to the ball bottom, then wrap and wire it evenly over the ball. Pull long sprigs over to fill empty areas and wire to secure.

2 Cut the ribbon into 18" lengths. Hold two raffia strands over one length and make into a 4½" long loop with a 6" tail. Wire to secure, then shred the raffia loops and tails with your fingernail. Repeat with the remaining ribbon lengths and raffia. Glue the loops evenly spaced over the ball, extending outward.

3 Cut the eucalyptus into 6"–6½" sprigs. Glue them evenly spaced over the entire ball, extending outward. Repeat with 5½"–6" linum sprigs.

4 Cut the plumosus into 7"–8" sprigs and glue evenly over the ball among all the materials. Cut the safflowers to 6"–6½" long. Carefully glue them evenly among all the materials, extending outward.

Happy Halloween

18" round grapevine wreath
two 5" tall purchased stuffed black fabric cats
10–12 strands of naturally colored raffia,
   36"–45" long
10"x5½" TWIGS™ fence
3⅝ yards of 1½" wide orange taffeta ribbon with
   gold wired edges
5 artificial pumpkin picks: 3 with three 1¼" wide
   pumpkins, 1 with a 1½" pumpkin and 1 with
   a 2" wide pumpkin
1 mixed silk flower bush in fall colors with 14
   branches of ¾"–3½" wide yellow/red and
   white blossoms plus many green leaves
4 oz. of naturally colored dried barley
white spray paint, 30-gauge wire
glue gun and sticks or tacky craft glue

1 Cut the binding vines or wires off the
wreath. Pull the wreath apart, pulling the
center vines toward the back and the outer vines
toward the front. Wire the top area, leaving the
bottom area loose and about 6" deep. Spray the
fence white and let dry. Wire it into the wreath
bottom, angled with the left side toward the
back and the right closer to the front.

2 Glue a cat in front of each end of the fence,
positioning the right one lower than the left
one. Cut the picks off all the pumpkins. Angling
them as shown, glue a 1¼" one on one side of
the right cat and a 1½" one on his other side. Glue a 2"
pumpkin to the right of the left cat. Cut a leaf and three
smaller flowers off the bush. Glue in a cluster next to one
cat's feet; repeat next to the other cat.

3 Cut the branches off the bush. Set one aside; glue the
rest to extend from the center top halfway down each
side of the wreath, overlapping and hiding the stems. Be sure
to alternate colors. Hold a raffia strand over the ribbon and
make an oblong bow (see page 20) with a center loop, ten
2½"–5" loops and 20" tails. Knot each ribbon tail 2" from the
end. Wire extra raffia tails under the bow, then glue the bow
over the stems at the center top. Weave the tails among the
flowers on each side. Cut the flowers from the last branch
into 3"–4" sprigs; glue above and below the bow.

4 Glue a 1¼" pumpkin below the bow center, then glue
three on each side, evenly spaced among the flowers.
Cut the barley into 4"–7" sprigs and glue evenly spaced
among the flowers. Glue three barley sprigs around the cats
as shown in the large photo above. Make six raffia loops,
each with six 3" loops and 5" tails (see page 119). Glue one
near each upper pumpkin. Shred the loops and tails with
your thumbnail. Make a wire loop hanger on the top back
(see page 12).

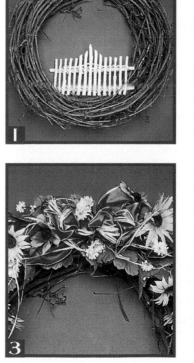

Magnolia & Sweet Pea Swag

30" lacquered vine swag
3¼ yards of 2⅞" wide purple wire-edged taffeta ribbon with a black sheen
4 oz. of naturally colored raffia
1 stem of white silk magnolias with five 2"–5" wide blossoms, 2 buds and 8 leaves
2 stems of magenta silk sweet peas, each with eight 2" long blossoms, 7 buds and many leaves
5 oz. of green preserved cedar
30-gauge wire
glue gun and sticks or tacky craft glue

1 Clip 20 twigs from the swag back, 9"–14" long, and set aside for step 3. Cut each sweet pea stem to 21". Wire end to end over the swag front, extending 2" beyond the swag ends. Cut the 5" magnolia blossom with a 1" stem; set aside for step 3. Cut the upper 12" of the remaining stem; wire it to extend to the left side among the sweet peas. Cut the rest of the magnolia stem to 11" and wire to the right side among the sweet peas.

2 Hold two raffia strands over the ribbon and handle as one to make an oblong bow (see page 20) with eight 4"–6" loops, an 11" loop to hang downward and a 7" tail. Shred the raffia loops and tails with your thumbnail, then glue the bow to the swag center.

3 Glue the 5" magnolia blossom under the bow, angled to the lower right, with a leaf on each side. Cut 5"–10" cedar sprigs and glue evenly spaced among the materials on each end of the swag. Glue 3"–4" sprigs around the bow. Glue the twigs from step 1 evenly among the materials on each end.

4 Hold three wide raffia strands together and make into 4" long loops with 4" tails. Secure with wire, then cut the loops to make the bundle all tails. Shred the tails. Glue the bundle behind the bow, extending upward and slightly left. Make six more bundles; glue three on each end, evenly spaced among the materials. Attach a wire loop hanger (see page 12) to the back of the swag.

A Bow Full of Roses

6 oz. of naturally colored raffia, 52"–56" long
3¼ yards of 1⅜" wide burgundy/black/gold floral
    printed ribbon
7 stems of red dried roses, each with a 1" long head
2 oz. of naturally colored dried brisa media grass
2 oz. of naturally colored dried floral buttons
1 oz. of green preserved plumosus
2 oz. of mauve dried pepper berries
24-gauge wire
glue gun and sticks or tacky craft glue

1 **To make the raffia bow:** Carefully divide the raffia into two equal bunches. Fold one bunch at the end to make an 8" long loop, leaving a 36" tail; wrap with wire to secure. Repeat with the other bunch. Place the wired areas together and wire to secure. Twist the wire ends to make a loop hanger at the back.

2 Use the ribbon to make an oblong bow (see page 20) with two 3", four 4" and two 4½" loops, a 20" tail and a 24" tail. Wire and glue to the raffia bow center. Cut the roses to these lengths: three 3", two 5" and two 7". Glue the 3" roses evenly spaced around the bow center, angled outward. Glue the 7" roses to the bow, one angled to the upper left and one to the lower right. Glue the 5" roses among the bow loops, one angled to the lower left and one to the upper right.

3 Cut the brisa media into 6"–10" sprigs. Glue them to the raffia bow extending outward from the center. Cut 4"–5" sprigs and glue among the ribbon bow loops. Repeat with the plumosus, spacing the sprigs evenly among all the materials.

4 Hold three floral buttons together and cut to 4"–5" long. Glue in a cluster to the bow, extending outward from the center. Repeat with the remaining floral buttons, cutting these 4"–8" long and spacing the clusters evenly among all the materials. Cut the pepper berries into 4"–6" sprigs and glue evenly spaced. (Be sure to wash your hands after handling the berries, as they contain a pepper-like material which can burn tender skin.)

The nine-foot PVC or vinyl pine garlands are wonderful and so very versatile for decorating throughout a house—and they can be very inexpensive! Loop a ribbon among the sprigs, gluing where necessary, then add sprigs of dried baby's breath or German statice. Place the garland on a mantle, then set a collection of vintage toys, or candles of varying heights, or even rustic birdhouses among the loops. Almost anything can be made festive with just a few inexpensive components strategically placed.

Choosing several ribbons which complement or coordinate allows more versatility in decorating throughout your house. Mix it up a little with varying components as well. As long as the pieces complement each other, the final outcome will be spectacular. Just make sure the colors blend, the style matches throughout and the placement of each design works. For instance, put the larger decorations in areas where they will be the stars of the room; allow room around them so they may be easily viewed. Smaller pieces become accents to bring the whole room together and fill empty areas with the colors of Christmas.

Several popular styles work well in Christmas decorating. Rustic, natural Christmas decorations, which include twigs, birds, dried filler flowers, pine cones, raffia, burlap ribbon and berries, are especially appropriate with the current interest in

environmental issues and the
general resurgence of a push back to
nature and things natural.

Another popular decorating style revolves around
the color combination of ivory and gold; put that together with
angels and you have a style! Something which works well with
ivory and gold is the snow or frost which is found on many vinyl
garlands or silk flowers and berries. They all function together to create an elegant, abundant feeling to Christmas.

Of course, good old fashioned red and green never goes out of style for
Christmas decorations. Whether it's centered around vintage toys, all
sorts of Santas and St. Nicks, or red and white poinsettias, this combination is always festive. Adding gold touches, such as a gold braid mixed in
with the other ribbons, or maybe a large jingle bell inserted into a collection, can brighten the whole look and give it a richness and a feeling
of warmth.

In this section we've shown several different styles. Choose the one
which best represents your feelings about Christmas and expand it to
include enough decorations for an entire room. You'll be surprised
how walking into a completely decorated room will affect your mood
at Christmas time. When done well, the feeling is one of welcome
and festivity—something we all cherish at this and any time
of the year!

Christmas Topiary

32" tall vine topiary on a log base
9' long vinyl evergreen garland
2⅔ yards of 2½" wide red/green/cream
Christmas print ribbon with gold wired edges
1 green silk holly bush with 5 branches, each
with 3 sprigs of seven 1½"–3" long leaves
and red berries
4 oz. of white dried statice sinuata
4 oz. of dried birch branches, 12"–18" long
24-gauge wire
glue gun and sticks or tacky craft glue

1 Fluff the garland. Wire one end to the top of the topiary ball, then wind the garland in a spiral around the ball, placing the rows 3" apart and using all the garland. Wire the other end in place.

2 Use the ribbon to make an oblong bow (see page 20) with a center loop, six 4"–4¾" loops, a 20" and a 34" tail. Glue it to the ball top with the short tail at the right. Loop the long tail down the left side, gluing to secure the loops. At the ball bottom, glue the tail next to the trunk and allow it to hang downward. Loop and glue the short tail over the right side of the ball to within 4" of the end.

3 Cut the holly branches off the main stem, then cut each into three 4" sprigs. Glue the fifteen sprigs evenly over the entire ball to extend outward.

4 Cut the statice into 4"–5" sprigs and glue them evenly spaced over the entire ball as shown in the large photo. Cut the birch branches into 5"–6" twigs; discard the heavy sections of the branches. Glue them extending outward among the evergreen sprigs and holly.

1

front view

2 left side view

3

4

Candle Centerpiece

32" long green vinyl fir swag with many 6" sprigs

3½ yards of 1¼" wide dark green velvet ribbon with gold wired edges

3½ yards of ⅜" wide gold wired braid

2 stems of pink/mauve silk hydrangeas, each with a 7" wide head of ¾"–2" wide blossoms and 9 leaves

4 mauve/green Christmas picks, each with a pink satin ball, three mauve berries, a mauve pine cone, 3 fir sprigs and 6 holly leaves

2 oz. of green preserved leatherleaf fern

½ oz. of naturally colored dried rice grass

1 green plastic candleholder with a 3" wide opening and prongs

3"x10" pink pillar candle

30-gauge wire, glue gun and sticks or tacky craft glue

1 Fluff the swag. Use wire cutters to trim ½" off the bottom of each candleholder prong. Cut a 12" length each of braid and ribbon. Glue the ribbon around the candleholder, aligning the gold edge with the holder edge. Glue the braid over the ribbon center. Apply glue to the inside of each prong and press the holder over the center of the swag, making sure the prongs go between sprigs to rest on the table.

2 Cut each hydrangea to 6" long and fluff out the blossoms and leaves. Glue one on each side of the candleholder extending toward the swag end. Cut the stem of each pick to 2½". Glue one in front of the candleholder and one behind it, angled in opposite directions. Glue another near each end of the swag.

3 Cut eight 14" lengths each of braid and ribbon. Hold each braid length over a ribbon length and handle as one to make a 4" ribbon loop (see page 21) with a 5½" tail. Secure with wire; trim the ribbon tail in a V and the braid tail diagonally. Glue one loop in front of and one behind the candleholder, angling them in opposite directions from the glued picks. Glue three loops on each swag end, alternating angles as shown.

4 Cut the fern into 4"–5" sprigs. Glue evenly spaced throughout the centerpiece, following the angles of the fir sprigs, as shown in the large photo. Cut 5"–6" rice grass sprigs. Glue them evenly spaced but sparingly throughout the centerpiece. Place a candle in the holder.

Pine & Oranges for Christmas

14" round straw wreath

4¾ yards of 2⅝" wide green/maroon/navy plaid wire-edged ribbon

1 oz. of naturally colored raffia

2 stems of green vinyl pine, each with twelve 5" long sprigs

1 stem of latex fruit with a 3" wide half apple, a 2" green pear, a 1¼" brown plum, a 2" maroon pomegranate, numerous burgundy, green and yellow 1"–2" blackberries and seven 2"–3½" wide gold-brushed grape leaves

six 2"–4" long naturally colored dried chili peppers

1 oz. of naturally colored dried baby's breath

five 3"–4" naturally colored dried orange slices

U-shaped floral pins

24-gauge wire

glue gun and sticks or tacky craft glue

an 11" and a 13" tail. Shred the raffia loops, then glue the bow over the pine stems at the center top.

1 Cut an 80" ribbon length and push a U-pin through one end to secure it to the upper back of the wreath. Wrap it in a spiral around the wreath, spacing the wraps evenly. Use your fingernail to shred two raffia lengths into thinner strands. Glue them over one ribbon end and wrap them over the ribbon around the wreath. Glue the strand ends at the back, trim the excess and continue with two more strands until you return to the starting point. Trim the excess and glue the ends to secure.

2 Trim the pine stems to 12". Place them end to end at the top of the wreath; U-pin in several places to secure. Hold two raffia strands over the remaining ribbon and handle as one to make an oblong bow (see page 20) with a center loop, two 3½", two 4¼" and two 5" loops,

3 Cut the large apple off the fruit stem and glue it under the bow. Cut the rest of the stem into two 8" sprigs with approximately equal amounts of fruit. Glue one on each side of the bow, extending over the pine and following the curve of the wreath.

4 Glue three chilies on each side, spacing them evenly and alternating the angles. Carefully break the orange slices in half. Glue one above the bow and one below the bow near the apple. Glue four slices evenly spaced on each side, alternating angles as shown in the large photo. Cut the baby's breath into 4"–6" sprigs; glue evenly spaced among all the materials and around the bow loops. U-pin a wire loop hanger (see page 12) to the upper back of the wreath.

Christmas Card Basket

14"x8"x6" whitewashed oval basket with a 15" tall handle

2⅔ yards of 2½" wide green/blue/maroon plaid taffeta wire-edged ribbon

1 maroon silk poinsettia bush with five 8" wide blossoms and many leaves

2 stems of green/blue/maroon blueberries, each with a 2" and a 3" wide head of many ⅜"–½" wide berries

2 oz. of green preserved tree fern

2 oz. of green sheet moss

3"x4"x6" block of floral foam for silks

30-gauge wire

glue gun and sticks or tacky craft glue

1 Trim the foam to fit at one end of the basket and extend 1" above the rim. Glue in place, then use a knife to trim the sharp upper edges. Cut a 10", an 11", a 12", a 13" and a 16" poinsettia stem. Wire the 16" and 13" stems to extend from 4" above the rim up the handle. Wire in several places to secure. Insert the 11" and 12" stems at the front and the 10" stem at the back of the foam.

2 Cut one berry stem to 16" and one to 11". Insert the 16" stem into the center to extend among the three upper poinsettias. Insert the 11" stem at the left to extend up the left handle between and below the 11" and 12" poinsettias.

3 Use the ribbon to make a puffy bow (see page 20) with a center loop, six 4" loops, a 20" and a 17" tail. Attach to a wood pick and insert into the foam right of the flowers. Ripple and glue the 20" tail across the basket front and the 17" tail across the back.

4 Cut two 22" fern stems. Insert one in front of and one behind the basket handle, curving both to extend among the upper poinsettias. Cut 9"–17" fern sprigs and insert among the flowers and berries. Cut 5"–8" sprigs; insert around the front and back of the foam and near the bow. Glue moss to cover any exposed foam.

An Elegant Pair

12"x12" reclining papier-mâché reindeer
10"x17" standing papier-mâché reindeer
3⅓ yards of ½" wide sheer gold ribbon with
  solid edges
2 stems of green vinyl noble fir, each with
  twelve 5" sprigs of ¾" long needles
1 stem of red berries with 16 clusters of five
  ¼" wide berries
1 stem of cream latex Japanese apricot blossoms with a 15" section of 1" wide flowers
  and ⅜" wide buds
4 stems of golden brown preserved eucalyptus
metallic gold spray paint
iridescent acrylic paints: charcoal, red-brown
sponge, paper plate, water
24-gauge wire, two 18" lengths of 18-gauge
  green cloth-covered wire
glue gun and sticks or tacky craft glue

1 Spray both reindeer heavily with gold. Mist the berry stem lightly with gold. Squirt a small puddle of charcoal paint onto the plate. Dampen the sponge, dip it into the paint and dab it onto the plate until very little paint remains on the sponge. Wipe each reindeer lightly with the sponge. Be sure to wipe away most of the paint so they have an antiqued look. Let the deer dry, then repeat with brown paint and let dry again.

2 Cut the sprigs off the fir stem. Place one next to the 18-gauge wire 1" from one end. Wrap 1" of the sprig stem around the wire to secure it. Repeat with another sprig, overlapping the sprigs slightly. Continue until all the sprigs are used—this makes a wired garland which is easy to fit around the reindeer's neck. Repeat with the other fir stem and wire length.

3 Cut the berry clusters each with a 1" stem. Glue half the clusters evenly spaced along each garland, at sim-ilar angles to the fir sprigs. Cut the apricot stem into sin-gle flower sprigs and double bud sprigs, each with a 1" stem. Glue half to each garland as for the berries.

4 Cut the eucalyptus into 3" sprigs. Glue evenly spaced into both garlands at similar angles to the other materials. Wrap a garland around each deer's neck and twist the wire ends together. Trim excess wire and tuck the ends into the sprigs. Cut the ribbon into two 60" lengths. Use each to make a puffy bow (see page 12) with a center loop, eight 1¾" loops and 12" tails. Glue one to each garland at the back of the deer's neck. Loop and twist a tail around each side of the garland, tucking it down and gluing it among the sprigs.

Shelf of Frosted Greens

12"x8" wood shelf
two 1½" tall wood candle cups
burgundy taper candles: one 10", one 12"
1½ yards of 2⅜" wide cream sheer striped
    wire-edged ribbon
1½ yards of ½" wide metallic gold looped
    braid
1 stem of white snow-glazed poinsettia with a
    6" wide blossom, a 1½" gold pomegran-
    ate, seven ⅜" wide white berries and
    many 3"–4½" long latex grape leaves
1 latex berry stem with a 1" raspberry, six
    ½" round red berries, and eleven 3"–5"
    long magnolia and grape leaves
1 stem of green vinyl fir with three 10"
    branches of six 5" long sprigs
1 oz. of naturally colored dried rice grass
burnt umber acrylic paint
acrylic gloss varnish
1" wide paintbrush
sandpaper, clean cloth
24-gauge wire
glue gun and sticks or tacky craft glue

1 Sand the shelf and wipe clean with the cloth. Mix ½ teaspoon of paint with 2 tablespoons of water. Paint this wash on the shelf and candle cups; let dry. Sand and wipe the shelf and cups again. Varnish them; let dry. Sand and wipe, then apply a second varnish coat; let dry. Glue the candle cups to the shelf center.

2 Cut the branches off the fir stem and shorten to 9". Set one aside; glue the others end to end across the shelf. Cut the poinsettia pick to 12". Glue it onto the shelf angled to the right with the blossom in front of the candle cups; tuck the stem down among the fir sprigs.

3 Hold the braid centered over the ribbon and handle as one to make an oblong bow (see page 20) with a center loop, two 2" and four 3" loops, and 12" tails. Glue it to the poinsettia stem left of the blossom. Loop a tail among the fir sprigs on each side of the shelf.

4 Cut the berry stem into two 5" sprigs. Glue one among the fir sprigs on each side of the shelf, each angled toward an end. Cut a 3-sprig section off the remaining fir branch and glue it between the candle cups extending upward at the shelf back. Cut the remaining sprigs apart and glue to fill any empty spaces as shown in the large photo. Cut the rice grass into 4"–5" sprigs and glue evenly spaced among all the materials, angled similarly. Insert the candles into the cups.

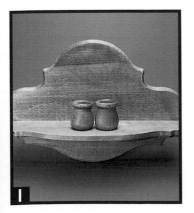

Gilded Poinsettia Wreath

- 20" green vinyl fir wreath with many 5" sprigs
- 3 ¼ yards of 2 ½" wide ecru/tan tapestry wire-edged ribbon
- 2 ¾ yards of ⅝" wide antique gold metallic wired braid
- 1 gold-brushed latex poinsettia/fruit stem with two 7" wide cream poinsettia blossoms, a 2 ¼" rust pomegranate, a 1 ½" burgundy apple, a 1 ¼" yellow apple, seven ¾"–1" various berries, and many holly and poinsettia leaves
- 5 oz. of dusty green preserved eucalyptus
- 2 oz. of naturally colored dried chesta
- 30-gauge wire
- glue gun and sticks or tacky craft glue

1 Cut the fruit stem to 21". Wire the stem end to the upper left of the wreath and curve it over the top. Pull the pomegranate and nearby leaves to extend downward over the stem, and shape the berries nearest the pomegranate toward the inside of the wreath.

2 Hold the gold braid over the ribbon and handle as one to make a puffy bow (see page 20) with a center loop, six 4½" loops, a 6" and a 24" tail. Glue the bow above the pomegranate. Loop and glue the long tails among the fir sprigs and fruit over the wreath top to the center of the right side.

3 Cut the eucalyptus into 6"–9" sprigs. Glue them evenly spaced following the shape of the wreath—notice that a 6" area at the center bottom is left empty.

4 Cut five 3"–4" sprigs each of eucalyptus and chesta; glue evenly spaced around the bow loops. Cut the remaining chesta into 4"–6" sprigs. Glue them evenly spaced among the eucalyptus and fir, following the same lines. Make a wire loop hanger on the back (see page 12).

Christmas Door Crown

32"x14" TWIGS™ wall plaque
1½ yards of 2½" wide burgundy/dark green/white Christmas printed ribbon with gold wired edges
2 stems of green silk pine, each with three 12" branches of five 5" sprigs and rope-wrapped stems
2 stems of burgundy fabric mums, each with a 5" wide blossom, a 2" wide bud and seven 3"–5" wired leaves
3 stems of dark red silk berries, each with 2 sprigs of ⅜"–⅝" berries and 1½"–3" long leaves
7 oz. of naturally colored dried canella pods (two 24" branches)
30-gauge wire, glue gun and sticks or tacky craft glue

1 Cut the 12" center branch off each pine stem; cut the rest of each stem to 17". Wire a 17" stem to each end of the crown over the straight bar, extending 2" beyond the end. Wire the 12" branches over the bar center, one extending toward each end, overlapping the stems 3".

2 Cut each mum into two 9" sprigs, each with a blossom or bud. Wire a blossom sprig on each side with the blossom positioned 7" from the crown center. Wire a bud on each end, positioned 6" past the blossom. Glue any leftover leaves around the blossom.

3 Tuck and glue the ribbon looping among the materials on the bar, with each end 2" from the end of the last pine sprig. Be sure to tuck the ribbon well down among the materials and bring the pine sprigs forward over it.

4 Cut two berry stems to 16". Wire one on each end of the crown to extend within 1" of the end of the last pine sprig. Cut the other berry stem into two 9" sprigs. Glue one extending over each 12" pine branch as shown in the large photo above. Cut the canella into 4"–5" sprigs. Glue them evenly spaced extending from the center toward each end.

Arch of Cedar & Roses

24" wide TWIGS™ arch with hanger

3⅓ yards of 1⅜" wide burgundy/green/mauve Christmas printed ribbon with gold wired edges

3¾ yards of ¼" wide mauve twisted satin cord

8 oz. of green preserved cedar

4 stems of mauve silk roses, each with a 4½" wide blossom and 3 wired leaf sprigs

3 burgundy/green Christmas picks, each with a gold-brushed burgundy apple, 2 cones, a cluster of gold berries, 3 pine sprigs and 3 holly leaves

30-gauge wire, glue gun and sticks or tacky craft glue

1 Set aside a 24" cedar branch for step 4. Glue the rest to the arch, extending 8" beyond the end of the twigs and covering the arch back to the center. Wire the stems if necessary for added security.

2 Cut two roses to 15". Glue and wire them to curve over each side of the arch, overlapping the stems 2" at the center top. Cut the other two rose stems to 7" and attach in the same way.

3 Use the ribbon to make an oblong bow (see page 20) with no center loop, ten 3"–4" loops and 19" tails. Glue to the arch center at an angle as shown, then loop and glue a tail among the materials on each side. Use the cord to make a loopy bow with six 3"–4½" loops and 40" tails. Glue this bow to the ribbon bow center. Drape and glue each tail in two 4½" loops toward the arch end.

4 Cut the stems of the picks to 2". Glue one on each side of the arch between the roses. Glue the last pick under the bow as shown. Cut the cedar branch from step 1 into 4"–7" sprigs; glue evenly spaced among the materials, extending forward, as shown in the large photo above. Cut 4"–6" baby's breath sprigs and glue evenly spaced along the arch, following the angles of the cedar sprigs. Glue short sprigs of cedar and baby's breath behind the bow extending up and down.

Fresh Greens for the Table

The types of fresh evergreens available vary by area; substitute as needed, and use trimmings from your Christmas tree. Using more than one kind of greenery adds texture and interest to your arrangements.

10"x2" dark-colored round plastic floral bowl
2" tall wood candle cup
12" tall dark red taper candle
2 yards of 1½" wide red/black lamé ribbon with gold wired edges
2 yards of ⅜" wide antique gold wired braid
fresh green branches: cedar, noble fir, Douglas fir
3 artificial berry picks, each with three 1⅜" long red raspberries, nine ⅜" wide red smooth berries and six 2"–3" long green latex leaves
1 silk berry stem with six 5"–8" long sprigs of ³⁄₁₆"–¼" red smooth berries
1 oz. of green sheet moss
4"x4"x3" block of floral foam for fresh flowers
two 2½" long wired wood picks
8" of 24-gauge wire
glue gun and sticks or tacky craft glue

1 Trim the foam to fit into the bowl, extending 1" above the rim. Glue in place, then trim the top edges so there is less to hide. Soak the foam in water until it is completely saturated. Use wire cutters to cut off the upper 1" of one wood pick. Glue the pick to the bottom of the candle cup, then insert it into the center top foam.

2 Cut 15 cedar branches to 11"–12" long. Insert around the sides of the foam extending outward over the table top, nearly hiding the bowl. Cut 10–12 noble and Douglas fir branches to 9"–10". Insert around the foam over the first layer. Repeat, cutting these 8"–9" long.

3 Cut 4"–6" sprigs of all the greenery. Insert around the candle cup extending upward and away from the cup, completely covering the foam top. Hold the braid over the ribbon and handle as one to make a puffy bow (see page 20) with a center loop, eight 3" loops and 5" tails. Attach to a wood pick and insert at the front next to the candle cup.

4 Trim the berry pick stems to 2". Shape the leaves and berries to curve naturally. Insert evenly spaced around the candle cup to extend outward. As shown above, cut the berry stem into six 5"–6" sprigs. Insert them evenly around the sides of the foam to extend among the greenery. Insert the candle into the cup.

Fresh & Festive Wreath

12" wire wreath—form with prongs

8"–10" fresh green branches: Douglas fir, noble fir, cedar

2 ⅞ yards of 2 ⅝" wide burgundy/gold tapestry ribbon with gold wired edges

6' long green silk holly vine with many ¾"–1" clusters of maroon berries and 1" leaves

2 stems of navy/burgundy/dark green silk cranberries, each with a 10" section of many ⅜" wide berries and wired leaves

6 Christmas picks, each with a 1½" burgundy apple, two 1"–1½" cones, pine sprigs and holly leaves

22-gauge wire

1 Cut the greenery into 5"–7" sprigs. Place three sprigs of varied types between one set of prongs on the wreath form. Bend the prongs tightly over the sprigs to secure them. For security, bend one prong angled upward and one downward.

2 Position the next cluster of sprigs between the prongs so they cover the stems of the first cluster. Bend the prongs to secure them. Continue around the wreath. Tuck the stems of the last cluster under the first cluster to hide them.

3 Trim the excess stem off the holly garland and wire one end of it to the upper right of the wreath. Place the garland around the wreath, wiring it to the sprigs to secure. Use the ribbon to make an oblong bow (see page 20) with a center loop, six 3"–4" loops, a 22" and a 28" tail. Wire the bow to the upper right, slightly angled toward the outer edge, with the long tail extending upward.

4 Trim each berry stem to 11". Wire one to extend above the bow, curving over the wreath. Wire the second to extend from below the bow, again curving with the wreath. Loop and wire a bow tail in each direction among the greens and holly. Trim the stems of the picks to 2". Wire one pick beside the bow center on the inside of the wreath. Wire the others evenly spaced around the wreath. Attach a wire loop hanger to the upper back.

A Swag of Greenery

fresh green branches: twenty 16"–23" long
  cedar and assorted firs
4¼ yards of cream pearl beads
3 yards of 4" wide ivory/gold tapestry ribbon
  with gold wired edges
1 white flocked silk poinsettia bush with at least
  four 8"–10" wide blossoms and many leaves
22-gauge paddle wire

1 Hold a 12" and a 23" cedar branch together end to end with the shorter one extending upward and wire together; do not cut the wire. Wire a 10" fir branch over the 12" cedar one. Place an 18", then a 16" fir branch over the 23" branch and wire.

2 Continue adding shorter branches to the upper and lower portions of the design as desired, securing with wire each time. Twist the wires together at the back and make a loop hanger (see page 12).

3 Cut an 8" wide poinsettia with a 4" stem and wire to extend upward over the greenery. Cut a 10" poinsettia to 16" long, another to 11" long and an 8" wide one to 9" long. Place the 11" stem over the 16" stem, angled left. Place the 9" stem right of the 11" stem; wire all the stem ends together, then wire them to the swag extending downward from the binding area.

4 Wire one end of the beads to the swag at the binding. Make two 18"–21" loops, wiring to secure each—do not cut the beads. Use the ribbon to make an oblong bow (see page 20) with a center loop, six 4"–6" loops, a 14" and a 21" tail. Wire it over the binding. Loop a tail down each side, tucking it among the greenery and poinsettias. Make three 7"–15" bead loops and wire to extend from beneath the bow over the poinsettias.

INDEX

(Bold print indicates project title.)